THE SAID SHE SAID
Single Men Talk About Dating New Millennium Women

Printed in the United States of America
Version I - 12/2017

ISBN-10:0-9990738-1-8
ISBN-13:978-0-9990738-1-0

Published by D.A. Brown Consulting dba Hoosevents, LLC
www.DABrownConsulting.com

I0081198

DISCLAIMER: The purpose of this workbook is to help those who desire to develop loving, healthy, relationships with others. This book should be used as an educational tool and while the concepts identified in this book are based on personal views along with psychological and coaching theories, no therapeutic benefits are offered or implied. Therapy and coaching sessions are a process that is offered between the professional and their client, the tools identified in this book can help individuals identify areas in their life they may need to re-evaluate and if the individual is not able to identify solutions by walking through this self-healing process, consult a therapist or a professional life/relationship coach who can help you work through some of the behavior issues identified. The reader should consult proper medical advice in matters relating to his/her mental health and particularly with respect to any symptoms that may require diagnosis or mental health attention.

Cover Design designed by Jason Harvey

Contact D.A. Brown Consulting for Relationship/Life Coaching services and Speaking Engagements:
Delbra Brown
Rochester NY 14606
(585) 317-4313
info@DABrownConsulting.com

Discount pricing offered to educational and organizational institutions that desire to use this self-help guide in volume or a group setting. Contact Mrs. Brown for details on volume pricing.

OTHER BOOKS AVAILABLE ON AMAZON.COM

Adult Edition

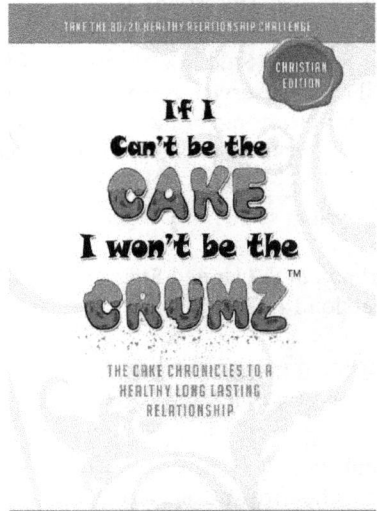

Christian Edition

Teen Edition

Table of Contents

Chapter 1 - *Are Men & Women Really Different?*

Table of Contents

Chapter 2 - *Rules of Dating*

Table of Contents

Chapter 3 – *Tips about establishing and maintaining a relationship*

Table of Contents

Chapter 4 – After the love is gone

Chapter 5 – Religion & Dating – Is it possible?

ACKNOWLEDGEMENTS

First giving honor to God who is truly the head of my life, home and being. It is because of Him I am taking the time to put together this book. It is truly a gift to be single in this day and age. And if you know your walk in Christ, you'll learn to listen to Him when He speaks and you'll find yourself stepping out on faith for all the things he asks for you to do, knowing that if you do, you'll never fail.

To my beautiful daughter, Karie. It is for you and my other adopted daughters that I write this book. God has directed my steps as a parent and I love the young woman that you are. I remember the story you told me about the boy in high school that offered to walk you to class and how you told him if he walked you to class, he'd be late for his and how you laughed it off with him and kept walking. I thank God that although my life hasn't been all that I expected, my love of God and my walk with Him has guided your steps and that's more than I can ask for in this lifetime! I love you more than life itself.

To my grandmother and family, though we have our times and moments, thanks for trying to be sure I understood how important it is for the family to stick together. I love you all and especially my grandmother.

To those whom I've loved and lost, I came to realize you can't lose what you never had. And though some of you may have gotten in the way of our building a great relationship had you been ready, I realize just how I may have gotten in the way when you thought you were. It is because of my life's journey in love and relationships that I write this book and I thank you for being you. You've helped me to understand why my sisters needed this information. And to the men that have allowed me the privilege of seeing dating, relationships, and love through your eyes, I thank you. Your desire to help me educate my sisters on how they too can get off the "Black Man's Buffet" and into healthy and productive relationships. Kudos to you all!!

Note: All of the bachelors lived in Rochester, New York at the time the questions were asked in 2004. Since that time, some of them no longer live in Rochester, NY, and at least one of them have passed away. I am grateful for the opportunity to have been their friend, and to have been entrusted with the information they shared with me. Ladies, use this as a guide to help you understand how to get to the truth from the men in your life. The answers the guys gave me may not be the thoughts, views, and opinions of "all men" or even "all heterosexual men," however it was a great way for me to hear their truth, and for me to understand my truth may not be someone else's and once I learned that, I had to then ask myself "now that you know how men think, what are you going to do about it?"

PROLOGUE (2004)

The comments made by the bachelors interviewed for this book were written and transcribed how the men shared them with me as this was an opportunity for single men to share their views and perspective on dating, love and relationships. This was their chance to give the "new millennium woman" some ideas on how to attract the man of her dream while at the same time, not lose sight of the woman she desired to be. By conducting the interviews with the bachelors, I grew in my understanding of men and what I may have been doing wrong when it came to my failed attempts to secure that "great relationship" I thought I was establishing. I write this book with the hopes and desire, that women and men look into their hearts and minds and learn how to appreciate the single new millennium woman who wants to be in a healthy relationship and not just played over like a toy.

Ladies, picture this! Imagine you're in a store, minding your business when a handsome man approaches you and asks for your name. In the time it takes for you to say your name, ask him his, and he responds, you've

1) reflected on the tone and pitch of his voice,
2) the words he used when he spoke,
3) checked out his height, physique, butt, legs, chest, hands, hair,
4) clothes coordination,
5) the type of shoes he's wearing,
6) and his lips.

And by the time he finally tells you his name, you've already decided whether or not he might get your phone number if he ask. Once you have exchanged numbers, the dating ritual has begun. Unfortunately, for many single ladies, their love life and dating has not been what they imagined it would be when they were a little girl. Women today are finding that the rules of engagement in dating have changed. Women went from being wives, taking care of their homes, the kids, and their spouses or mates, to women fighting for total equality in all things that a man was given. The right to vote, to have equality at work, equal pay, and even equality in her sex lives. Women today are encouraged to be educated, to stand up for what they believe in, to challenge society, and the men in their life, and live as if the word "no" is no longer the only option. With this mindset, women find themselves reinventing the rules of dating without even knowing what the rules are.

As young girls grew into young women, they no longer wanted to just please their man. They also want to receive pleasure and they desire to be comfortable exploring their own sexuality. Over the course of time, today's woman became self sufficient, independent, great cooks, great moms, and began to have great sex lives, but somehow in the new millennium (2000+), they've found themselves still single and not understanding why? They're holding it down when it comes to taking care of business; personally, professionally and sexually, but single men today of all ages don't find them interesting enough to build long lasting relationships with.

PROLOGUE (2004) - *continued*

They find them good enough to bed, but not to wed. Good enough to date, but not to mate or to marry. So the question they find themselves asking is "What is really the problem?"

In 2004 I was single and not sure what I was doing wrong in my dating practice so I decided to interview a few single, uncommitted bachelor men and ask them the questions I felt every woman would want to know. Although I never got the chance to finish asking them the 70 questions I outlined, I am publishing their answers in this reality reading forum hoping that women will be encouraged to read their views and perspectives on dating, love and relationships. They did the interviews with me to help the "new millennium woman" get realistic ideas about how men perceive their actions, and what they can do to help land the man of her dreams. It is my hope and desire, that this book helps women look into their hearts and minds and learn from the knowledge shared by the men like it significantly helped me.

It is now 2017 and almost 13 years since I interviewed the bachelors. I learned a great deal from the men. I asked direct questions and they were honest with me and I LOVED them for it. Over time, I understood why relationships are so complicated and from the knowledge and information I obtained, I wrote my first book The Cake Chronicles 80/20 healthy relationship guide titled, *"If I Can't Be The Cake, I Won't Be The Crumz."* In order to bake a great cake, you have to have the right ingredients and a relationship is like having a great cake. You have to define what you want to be happy or your 80% and what you are willing to compromise, or your 20%. The men helped me realize there is a great deal that goes into relationships and because of that revelation; it was my quest that women are provided the tools to understand the work that is needed in order for them to establish an ideal one.

PROLOGUE (2017)

It is now thirteen (13) years since I interviewed and gleaned from the bachelors the knowledge and wisdom which inspired me to go on a personal quest to identify exactly the challenges women face in establishing healthy, long lasting relationships with others. Over the years, I came to realize it is not enough to tell us that it takes a lot of work to maintain the relationship once you have one; but we need to understand exactly what that "work" entailed. God granted me my wish and as He guided me to the knowledge and wisdom I needed to uncover the tools that are needed, I applied them to my life and they helped me change how I engaged others when establishing a relationship with them. It was not enough for me to learn what was needed; I had to learn how to think and respond to people "differently" if I was going to succeed. And even though I realized I initially didn't know where to begin, after my discussion with the bachelors, one night God woke me up at 3:00 am to watch a television program where a woman was talking about "dysfunction." That was a term I had never heard before but one I would become intimately educated about. The dialogue the ladies were having peaked my interest and as I woke up to search the Internet for books to explain what it was, the books God directed me to discover led me on a lifelong journey to understand why relationships are so complicated and 13 years later, using my grandmother's wisdom and the knowledge I uncovered, I produced *the Cake Chronicles "If I Can't Be The Cake, I Won't Be The Crumz" 80/20 Healthy Relationship Self-Help Guide.*

The book helps women identify the ingredients and the knowledge that is needed to change their views about relationships and to discover how to truly "Act Like A Lady, But Think Like A Man." However, the real reason I went on that journey was because of the men who graciously shared their "truth" with me. In order for women to understand why I understand men, they needed to see what men really thought about women so this book was written to help women realize how men pay closer attention to us than we do to ourselves. When women learn how to read them like they read us, we will be able to see if the person in your life is for you or against you. You don't have to wait for them to hurt you. You will learn the necessary tools that are needed to allow friends and family members in your circle, and create healthy, firm boundaries with frenemies and relatives. May you be educated and blessed as I was about who I call the "men people," and may you obtain a greater appreciation for the differences that exist in some men while at the same time; you learn how to support and appreciate them for who God has designed them to become I pray you understand the power women have in contributing to them becoming greater because of our influence.

ABOUT THE AUTHOR
2004

As a child growing up in the 70's, my mother used to tell me while ironing our clothes on a clear Saturday afternoon in the summertime, "Delbra, don't depend on no man. Be self sufficient and independent. Make your own money, that way, can't no man tell you what to do!" I remembered her getting up at 4:30 am to fix our breakfast and leave it in the oven keeping warm until we woke up to go to school all before she went to work. She taught me how to take care of my brothers, to cook for the family when I came of age, and she taught me to love my family. She gave me everything I needed to take on the world except the foundation for establishing a healthy relationship. Unfortunately, she couldn't teach me that, because she didn't have a good foundation herself. My parents divorced when I was young. From the age of five until I was 25, I had a step-father that was physically, emotionally, psychologically, and mentally abusive. He did the best he could, but it just wasn't good enough. His parenting style was old-fashioned because he believed that everyone in the house was to do as he said, and not as he did. Before he went to work, he would drop my brothers and I off to my grandmother's house in Hanover Projects and let my grandmother and the neighborhood raise us while my mother was at work. During the times when he wasn't working, he would curse everybody in the house out, and start beating on us after he'd come home from a bad day of chilling in the streets, so I spent most of my teenage years wondering why did we have to be subjected to that. Adults need to understand they are their children's first instructors and their children will learn from them about life from them whether it's good or bad, or whether they're in the home or not. Parents are the primary influencers of how their children will be prepare for relationships, love, marriage and life. Growing up during the 70's – 90's, I was determined to be treated as a man's equal. I wouldn't walk behind him, but beside him. I would become that self sufficient, independent woman my mother talked about while at the same time, obtain that loving husband and the relationship I knew I deserved to have. When I was younger, I married my daughter's father, and looking back on things now, he loved me as best he could. I realize now, that my independence and lack of knowledge about men got in the way of my seeing that his way to show love was different than what I wanted. I didn't know how to interpret his intentions and actions as love because I had my own preconceived idea of what I and how he was "supposed" to show love. So when he didn't do what I wanted him too, I thought he must not have loved me as I did him. It took me from the time we separated and got divorced, until I was 38 before I realized he did in fact love me. It took more than five years after my interview with the bachelors for me to truly understand what men really want from women. I always thought men and women wanted the same thing. You know, we both have a mother and a father; therefore he should be able to relate, and understand me. I now realize society has encouraged women to lower or not have any standards at all, and in doing so, there are a lot more single beautiful women holding down their households, wanting love but not in love. And even though women outnumber men, there are a lot of great single men not in relationships because of the lack of standards in women.

ABOUT THE AUTHOR
2017 & Beyond

From 2004 until 2008 I tried and put the theories I had for relating to others to the test. I realized I never knew I had permission and the authority to define boundaries when someone intentionally or unintentionally did or said something to hurt me. I tested the men in my life and to my surprise, what I desired to have in my relationships started happening. I no longer waited for someone to get the memo. I ensured they did. I no longer say the words "I think," "maybe," "I don't know," and "I'm not sure." If I don't know, I ask. If I'm not sure, I don't lie and say anything to please others. I tell them I'm not sure and I wait to see if they want me to help them find a solution. I don't volunteer just because someone looks like they are in need. I learned how to say no. And I learned boundaries. All of this was done because I learned how to accept the fact that I matter and it is not up to others to show or tell me that. I have all the power that is needed to embrace that philosophy. I now know it starts and ends with me.

This book is written to help women understand the differences that exist between what women think and believe about relationships than what men do. This book will help women understand what men really want in their dates, mates and wives and once women understand how to stand firm and comfortable raising the bar from our men so there can be a lot more relationships in the country, than booty call dates or as they say "dates on rotation." This book is not to be considered a standard for everyone, but for those who are interested in having a productive, healthy, relationship, this is for you!

ABOUT THE BACHELORS

About Bachelor #1

Bachelor #1 was 38, born in Rochester, N.Y. Parents were born in Pompano, Florida and Kingstree, S.C. He was raised in Rochester by his parents. He has been married twice; once when he was 24 and then we he turned thirty. He had one daughter and one baby momma. He had dated 200 women and has sex with all 200 hundred. He has only been serious with 3 of them. Both his parents talked to him about dating and he has talked with his child about dating as well. Hi uncles talked with him about dating and he also learned about it from watching television, books and what he saw from other relationships around him.

About Bachelor #2

Bachelor #2 was 38, born in Syracuse New York. His mother was born in New York, but his father was born in Florida. He was raised in Rochester, NY mostly by his mother and his aunt and uncle. He was married once at 26 and has 2 kids with 2 baby mommas. He had dated approximately 300 women, had sex with approximately 200 of them, and he has only been serious with three or four of them. He has spoken with his children about dating, but he was never told by family members about it. He mostly saw things on T.V, movies, and through family members. Most of the men in his family were pimps, players and hustlers so he saw them pimpin beautiful women. These were beautiful women who gave them money and kept these guys in cars they didn't work for. To me, there was nothing better in the world than being a pimp. You got beautiful women, you got money, you got cars you got access to sex whenever you want it. My mother would tell me don't be like the, but as children, you don't do as you're told, you do as you see. When I asked him if he was influenced by his friends or homeboys, he stated although they all had their versions of what dating was, it never was about dating. You played like you were dating to get what you wanted, but it wasn't dating. It was always about getting the pussy.

About Bachelor #3

Bachelor #3 was age 34, born in Rochester, New York. His parents were born in West Virginia and Georgia. He was raised in Rochester, NY and he attended college but never obtained a degree. He is a member of a church, has never been married, and has 1 child with 1 baby momma. He was 18 when he started having sex although he's dated older women with as much as 10+ years older than him and as young as 7 years. He's dated approximately 30 women, had sex with approximately 40 women and has as 10+ years older than him and as young as 7 years. He's dated approximately 30 women, had sex with approximately 40 women and has only been serious with 5. He hadn't begun to speak with his child about dating because he's very young but says he will. Neither his mother or family members talked to him about dating but he will talk with his son once he gets older. He has talked about dating with his friends but the primary source of his knowledge is from T.V. and movies. His highest gross earnings have been $26,000.

ABOUT THE BACHELORS - *continued*

About Bachelor #4

Bachelor #4 was age 24 and was born in Syracuse, New York. His parents were born in Auburn and Syracuse New York. He was raised in Rochester, N.Y primarily by his mother. He has never been married, isn't a member of a church, has a college degree, his financial earnings have ranged from $25,000 - $70,000. He has two children and one baby momma. He was 13 when he started having sex, has dated 200 women, and he can't remember how many women he has had sex with. The oldest was 21 years older than him, and the youngest was 2 years younger. He has only been serious with 10 of those women. He hasn't discussed dating with his children and his parents have never talked to him about dating but he was educated by an older friend. He obtained most of his knowledge about dating from television and other adults in his life. He is very interested in establishing a serious relationship.

About Bachelor #5

Bachelor #5 was age 36 and was born in Gary, Indiana. His parents were born in Chicago, Illinois, but he was raised primarily in Gary, Indiana by his parents, step-parents and grandparents. He isn't currently a member of a church. He has been married and has a child. He estimates he's dated at least 125 women. He was 13 when he first started having sex. The oldest woman he's dated was 20 years older and the youngest was 22. He couldn't remember how many women he has had sex with or how many of them he was serious with. He's talked to his child about dating and his parents and other adults around him did talk to him about it. He says he's learned a lot about dating from his sister and her friends. He says sometimes he's interested in having a relationship. He doesn't have a college degree and his declined to state his highest earnings to date.

.

Chapter One

Are Men & Women Really Different?

Chapter One
Are Men & Women Really Different?

In 1992, Dr. John Gray published a book titled *"Men Are From Mars, and Women Are From Venus"* suggested that men and women were "different." As I had been struggling to maintain a "healthy" relationship with the opposite sex, when I thought about the title, I said to myself "No Kidding!" Even though the title of the book modeled the challenges I was experiencing in my dating life, in the early 90's, I didn't think the book could provide information that would help me understand them better. However; over the years, as I experienced trials and tribulations in my dating practices I began to wonder exactly what I was doing wrong but I didn't have enough knowledge and information to change my dating habits. In 2002, my daughter was in her first year of college in North Carolina so my mother and I decided to give her a car, but we needed to deliver it to her in North Carolina and that meant we'd have to leave Friday morning, drive eleven and a half hours then turn right around on Sunday and drive back home before we both needed to get back to work. Because both my mother and I were single at the time and my mother was raising my nieces and nephew, we would have to take the children with us on the trip because we didn't have anyone else to watch them while we were gone. I realized it would be a difficult trip taking small children on a trip like that, but we did think it would be a great opportunity to share with them where their big cousin was going to school, but I realized we needed help so I decided to ask a male friend of mine if he would go on the trip with us to help us drive. He told me we shouldn't take the kids because it was not a "family vacation" but a trip that needed for us to just get there, and turn around and get back. At the time, it didn't seem like he understood why we would take the children on such a trip and because he wasn't trying to be "understanding" about our family dynamics which dictated our need to take the children, I found myself upset about his lack of "empathy" so we ended the conversation on bad terms. The next day I talked with another male friend about our decision to take the children on this road trip, and almost verbatim he told me the same thing my friend had said the day before so just like the previous conversation, we also parted ways on bad terms. They say three strikes and you're out, so I decided to talk with one other male friend about our plans to see if I could get some sympathy from a man about our decision, and he too said the same thing. It was in that moment that I realized there had to be something I was missing when it came to how men and women thought about situations. As I reflected on my conversations with three different guys who were of different ages, lived on different sides of town, who had different educational background yet were people I respected, I realized there was something unique about the guys I had in my life. Most men I have ever dated were what people called "a man's man," and because I was single, I thought it would be a great idea to truly understand if men and women were really different so I decided to put together a list of questions I would ask single men about love, life, and relationships. The first set of questions I asked the men were just basic questions and gave me the opportunity to just get inside their head.

Chapter One - *Are Men & Women Really Different?*

Question 1: What's a man/woman?

Bachelor #4 response: A man is a person that stands up for who he is, what he is, and what he does. He takes full responsibility for his actions. He knows what he's doing, and he doesn't jeopardize himself or those around him for petty gain. A man is someone that you look up to, not at. A woman is a compliment to a good man. She's everything a man is. She's a powerful individual with an opinion. She's beautiful both internally and externally. She's feminine. My mother's a woman; a great woman.

Bachelor #5 response: The Bible defines a man as a male that develops not just because he's at the age of majority, but because he decides to walk and carry himself as a man. He accepts his responsibilities. He accepts his burdens in life. He moves forward, and he progresses when it comes to his children. He's there to rear his children. He's there to be responsible for his children. He's there to protect his children. He's there to protect his wife, and he's there to build a life, and a lifestyle. A woman is essentially the same thing. She's there to raise her children, to protect her husband, protect her children, to establish a lifestyle, and to fulfill the need of that man. She has just as much responsibility as that man. Actually, she has more responsibility because one of the primary functions of a mother is to be the primary teacher of the children. That's her first job because she's the very first teacher those children have ever had because she carried them. So the things that she puts into her body and her mind are automatically distributed down to those children; so if she fills her mind and her body with junk, then she's filling her children with junk before they've had a chance to mature. I know my answer is going to have a lot of women pissed off, because they're going to be saying "what kind of man is he? How he gone say that about women?" Well, maybe women need to take a look at, or think about what I just said, and maybe they need to reassess because one of the reasons I feel we have a high rate of ADHD and we have so many children on Ritalin and all this other kind of B.S. is because of the lifestyle of some of these parents. There are mothers who are 4, 5, or 6 months pregnant in the clubs and bars. What are you doing pushed up at the bar with your belly drinking a beer, drinking a cocktail, and you got a 6 month baby in your stomach? You still trying to smoke a joint, wanting to be around folks that are smoking, constantly smoking either weed, cigarettes, or other stuff, but you can't figure out why your children are going to kindergarten and can't sit down, and you know in the first 5 years of their life, you've never really cooked them a full meal. Their first full meal came from McDonalds and was a happy meal. We've got to get back to the business of raising our children. We have too many children on Ritalin. We have too many children that are drug addicts before they get to the third grade.

Chapter One - *Are Men & Women Really Different?*

Question 2: Do you think men and women are different?

Bachelor #1 response: "Yes I do. Uh, women are more sensitive, more emotional, more uh, grounded. Men are free spirited, don't show their feelings too much. Secretive. Basically big punks at heart and looking for somebody to love them and nurture them.

Bachelor #2 response: He responded by sharing a story about a date he had on a Friday night with a younger woman. He told her "what's interesting about dating younger women is you recognize the game signs long before they come at you. I usually try to pump the brakes and say you know what? The game you trying to run on me, I taught them niggas how to run on you. That you know, you aint' getting nuttin over on me because what you fail to realize is, the one thing you countin on to get you what you want, every other woman in the world has that. There's nothing exclusive about it. Everything you may think you are used to doing, don't mean nothing to me. I've known someone that has done it. I may know two women who can do it. I may know two women in the world who'll do it at the same time, so don't bet the farm on that! I think that's where a lot of women mess up at. Thinking that their sexuality or sensuality will get them what they want. What I realize is that often times; their greatest asset is their greatest popularity point which is their femininity. Men are not looking for competition; men are looking for someone that's complimentary. Men date women that make them feel good about themselves. That's what attracts women to him, and what women fail to realize, is men are looking at how you make me feel when I'm going through tough times. When something's bothering me, how do you read me, how do you relate to me? I've often said the woman for me is smarter than me. She makes me think it's my idea when it's her idea. She basically knows how to stroke and prop up my ego but that's what men are looking for. One way or the other they're going to get it. In the new millennium, many men date a composite woman. One woman may cook well; one may clean well. There are different things about them to different people. If you break 'em apart and put them together, you'll have the perfect woman. The problem is, men are looking for perfection. They don't like to settle. Where a woman is different is they will settle all the time, because they are looking to try to fix the man; so we're looking from two totally different perspectives. Where we are so different is men are reared toward conquest, competition, who's the strongest, you know like how little boys are into violence and cars. We're into guns, playing football, and competitions. We're into being the best and having the most. Unlike women who are raised into being monogamous. You know playing dress up, playing with dolls, playing house, you know; um to be in love. To be with one guy.

Chapter One - *Are Men & Women Really Different?*

Unlike men who basically are taught to get as many knots as you can on your belt. So the whole sociology factor is where we are two totally different adults. As we grow up, we eventually want the same thing. Men attract women who are competitive, they got nice bodies, they're successful they dress nice; they have nice cars, and all the things they played with as boys. As for women they are out there looking good, they dressing themselves up, they got a nice new house, you know they acting like a lady so we are adults who basically are just stretched up and grown up. But we've been reared in two totally different directions. So what happens is that you basically have men who are taught we have to exchange love for lust. So I fake like I love you to get the lust I want. Women are taught to give him the lust he wants to get the intimacy she want. See we have to exchange that love for lust. And so what happens is that everyone is kinda playing the game. She may not really be in the mood to have sex, but she wants to be held and pampered so she knows okay, if I let him get off, then hopefully he'll hold me for a while, talk to me, just give me the comfort I need. He knows, if I hold her, kiss her on her forehead, talk to her, and say the right thing, that's gonna give her the comfort she needs so she can give me the sex I need. So it' an exchange where men and women are consistently going back and forth. It's like a ping pong game; but the thing is, they both are looking to get something totally different out of it. She is looking to get love, relationship, and a commitment out of it. He looking to get basically a no strings attached booty call out of it so the actions are the same, but the whole focus is two totally different outcomes.

Bachelor #3 response: Without a doubt. Psychologically our souls are different. Women are more emotional overall. Men are not. We're created for different roles so overall we are different.

Bachelor #4 response: No, I think our core values are the same, we just have different methods of expressing ourselves.

Bachelor #5 response: Yes. Their mindsets are different. Men naturally are conquerors. Women are nesters which mean they want to set up homes, have and raise children, and be family oriented. Men want to have a nice comfortable place to call home, but we need to have our wandering space. We're not necessarily doing anything that we don't have any business doing, but we want to just have our space to wander and women don't understand that. They think if we're not with them, then we're doing something wrong or we're trying to find another place to call home, and that's not always the case. You have some women now who feel that they've evolved so much that they've actually fooled themselves into thinking that they don't want to be in a relationship. They want to run

Chapter One - *Are Men & Women Really Different?*

around and act like men. The only reason I say that is their whole idea of what relationships are. Raising children are different, sexual encounters are different because now they consider them almost like conquests. They're proud of the number of men they've slept with, did this with, and got this from and let's be honest, our society has not changed that much. Women shouldn't be so proud of those little tid bits.

Question 3: What are some things men and women should know about each other?

Bachelor #1 response: Nothing, nothing at all.

Bachelor #3 response: Women um, once again are more emotional than guys so a lot of men should know that because of how society is. A lot of women have been hurt. A lot of women need someone to understand what they've gone through and that should also be vice a versa. Women should understand what men have gone through. It's not black or white. Um, women tend to think a little more with their hearts. Men don't, so men and women should try to understand each other. It's not hard. Women are not from Venus, and men are not from Mars. If truly someone loves somebody, they should try to understand them.

Bachelor #4 response: They know what they want within the first 5 minutes of meeting you. They make their mind up about what role you're going to play with them. No means no, unless it's given in a suggestive context. You know, sometimes when people say no, but they really don't want to say no, one of those it's too soon, but I really don't want you to stop, so I'ma say no, because I'm suppose to, but I really, really don't want you to stop, so if you keep going, I'm not going to say no again, but I gotta have it on the record that I did say no the first time. You tell that they don't mean no by not stopping immediately and at least 2 no's, really mean no.

Bachelor #5 response: If I knew that!

Question 3: What are some things women should know about men

Bachelor #1 response: That we are men and the average man is not a real man, he's still trying to figure out what a real man is. A real man is spiritually grounded. A real man has a fear of God and if he really doesn't he's lying to himself. In order for you to become a true man, you have to love the Lord and have a good Bible guideline because the Bible tells you how to truly be a man. Like love thou spouse, we are made in his own perfect image, and so if I'm made in God's own

Chapter One - *Are Men & Women Really Different?*

perfect image, I have to love my wife, and love whoever I'm with as God would love them, you know unconditionally.

Bachelor #3 response: Women should know that they don't think like men. And going back to that, women should take the time to understand whatever her man has gone through in his lifetime experiences. Um, and that goes with women also. Everyone has gone through experiences so women should also want to know what her man or the man she's interested in has gone through. Every man has a different experience.

Bachelor #4 response: Women should know that we're only going to do what you let us do. That you're probably never gonna get 100% of us no matter how hard you try. There's always a percentage that we keep to ourselves. Women should know we lie. We're hardly ever truly satisfied. Our ego usually thinks for us. 80% of us are materialistic, 90% of us are superficial, half of us have not learned how to get in touch with our feminine side, and express that in a way that doesn't create homophobic thoughts. As to men lying, if we're 10 minutes late from coming home, and the true reason is we stopped at the corner store to get a drink, and we don't want you to know, we gone lie about that. If we get a phone call from one of our home boys, and we don't want you to know, we lie about that. I think men are susceptible to lie about just about anything especially if they see it in their benefit. As to superficial, I mean, everybody want a trophy. I think all men want a trophy. More times than not, we look for what we think everybody else is looking for and not necessarily what we want for ourselves. As for femininity, it's hard to relate to anything if you don't allow yourself to fully understand it, and the only way you're going to understand the femininity of a woman is to get in touch with your own feminine side. A man can do this by allowing himself to cry every now and then. Allow himself to be sensitive about being soft. Allow himself to look at things from a less than masculine stand point. Stop thinking with this ego.

Bachelor #5 response: Men, don't always want what they ask for. Because we ask you to do a three way, maybe you shouldn't do it. Because maybe, that's not what we really want you to do. Because for one, that's not the woman 9 times out of 10 we are going to choose to be our wife. If a man tells you "oh baby I love you, I want you to have my baby," don't be stupid. Because, he may or may not be there, but you, definitely got a kid, and all of a sudden, he don't remember that conversation. And three, stop trying to compete for him. Stop trying to compete with other women for him. If you're the one he's going to choose, then you're the one he's going to choose. It's that simple. So you don't have to go out and sell yourself, market yourself, sacrifice your job, your income, your household to try and

Chapter One - *Are Men & Women Really Different?*

lure him from another woman. If he wants you, then you're the one he's going to choose.

Question 4: What is a man's ego and how important is it for him in determining a mate?

Bachelor #5 response: I think a man's ego can get in the way of a relationship if he feels like he's prettier than the woman he's dating, or if he feel more important than the woman he's dating. Some people consider it ego, some people call it self-esteem. Now a person with a real big ego will walk into a room and feel like the whole world is suppose to stop because he walked into the room. That's a person with a huge ego so pretty much anybody he's involved with is always going to be overshadowed by his own ego and his own personality. Now a person with a self-esteem problem, it doesn't matter who the woman is that he's with, he's always going to be uncomfortable because he's always feeling like he's not good enough to be with this particular woman. So every time she walks off he's trying to be right behind her because he feels like she's doing something or she's trying to find somebody to replace him. It's not so much that it's a jealousy thing, as it is an insecure thing. See jealousy is a little bit different. Jealousy means he just don't trust nothing she does. Esteem and ego play huge parts in relationships because you don't want to have such a huge ego that the person your involved with feels insignificant and you're attacking their self-esteem. Yet, at the same time, you don't want to be one of those people that's moping around and so uncomfortable with yourself that no matter who the woman is or what the woman looks like, you feel like you never measure up.

Question 5: If someone talked to you about dating, what things were you told?

Bachelor #1 response: Uh, don't spend no money on no woman. Don't try to bed em down (don't sleep with em on the first date). Always wear a condom. Never, never , ever, ever, ever, ever let em know how much money you got. Um, always let 'em go in their pocket first before you go in yours. If they don't open the door for you after you open the door for them, take 'em back home. You know stuff like that.

Bachelor #3 response: Uhm, how to treat a woman, a lady. Manners, how to be polite, and how to have etiquette around women like holding doors and stuff like that. I got that stuff from TV. As far as the guys I grew up with, they were more trying to be like the men so things were more around

Chapter One - *Are Men & Women Really Different?*

sex and we learned romantic stuff like giving 'em flowers and stuff like that. That's what I was taught.

Bachelor #4 response: Every relationship is different. You can't base a future relationship on a past relationship although it may have similarities. Every relationship is very unique in and of itself. Never put a stipulation or an expectation on a relationship 'cause it may be fortunate to be something that it wasn't necessarily destined to be. Let it take its natural course. Don't look for a relationship. Relationships are formed in and of themselves. When you try to form a relationship, you're probably likely to create something that isn't meant to be, and therefore you set yourself up to be in a very negative situation.

Bachelor #5 response: I remember I met this guy once, and one of the things he told me was, never give a woman everything. Always leave her wanting something, because if you give her everything, and she keeps on wanting more, what more will you have to give her. That sticks out to me because he was an absolute stranger and the conversation just came up. I was about 15 maybe and I just happened to be on the bus with a buddy of mine and that was the tip the old man gave me. It's made me a stingy bastard today. What I find is if you keep giving and giving and giving, if you're with the wrong person, she keeps taking and taking and taking, a lot of times, she's only asking to see how much more you're going to give. So if you don't have limits, why would she, so basically, don't let yourself be played out like a fool is what it really comes down to. Understand where you're trying to take this relationship to, and understand what you will, and will not do for it. More importantly, know your limitations. If you can't afford to do it, why are you trying? And if you can't afford to do it, and you keep on doing this, that, and the other, and she keeps on having more and more expectations, then maybe something should click in your head that she's playing you because she's not returning anything to you. I was also told, always treat a woman with respect and at the same time, make sure that she respects you. You find out if she respects you through her doing simple things. If you do nice things for her, and she has to think about whether she should do nice things for you, then she 'bout don't respect you. So I always deal with people who you can respect and who can respect you.

Chapter One - *Are Men & Women Really Different?*

Question 6: *What are some do's and don'ts men/women should look for?*

Bachelor #1 response: For men: The don'ts is: if you take a woman out to eat and she won't eat, that's a no no cause that means she's perpetrating. She frontin because later on that night you gone hear her stomach growling and what not. You know she's trying to front like she don't get her grub on. To me, that's you pretending all ready and you're lying to me, so to me your frontin so that's a definite out of the question. A woman that's afraid to pass gas in front of me, she fronting. A woman that's scared to burp and all that, you frontin. And to me that's like you're hiding in some kind of closet or playing some kind of game. And uh, then the other don'ts is um, if a woman does not every now and then want to offer to buy a brother dinner, she's out of the picture too. She's striking out right there. A woman shouldn't feel that a man have to cater to her every need. I don't play that. The do's: A woman should at least offer every now and then to buy dinner because me myself, I would never allow her to, but if she offered, that's a plus to me. A woman that would not necessarily break wind in front of me but say you know, she'd say excuse me I got to go in the other room because I got to do something you know, but if she did, I would find that so, to me, that that's sexy. Because in all honesty that means she's comfortable enough around me to do what she got to do you understand what I'm saying. I would appreciate that. That's about it. Don'ts a woman should look for in a man, I would honestly, say is if I was a woman, I would look for that fact if a man don't take the time to bless his food, that's a no no. If a man don't basically ask you what you want, where you want to go, and I'm not saying he got to cater to your every desire; but if he took the time to ask you out, then, let him take you out where you want to go. The don'ts; don't look for a brother to always get in your pants on the first date. Even if you truly want to. Don't allow him to take you there. You take him there. Other don'ts, uh, finances, the first date can be dutch. A brother won't lose respect for you if you go dutch on the first date. That means basically, cause the average brother thinking if he's paying for it, he gone get some skins on it. If you go dutch, then he knows right away. You can tell by his reaction if you decide to go dutch what his whole mentality is cause the average brother is gone be like nah baby I got this don't worry about it.

Bachelor #3 response: Men should look for if the woman or lady is insecure with herself or not. If she's been hurt, or a wounded angel. That may be somebody they maybe not want to mess with. Somebody that has not taken the time to heal yet. If the lady shows any signs of that, he should take his time, because not every woman is the same. A lot of women that have gone through a lot of stuff just need a man whose understanding. And then there's those women who are just not ready to

Chapter One - *Are Men & Women Really Different?*

date because they have not come to term with whatever they're burdens of the past are like unforgiveness, or whatever; so a man should really look out for that. Um. along those lines, insecurities in women where a woman might just be looking for a guy who just has money or potential as far as finances or just prosperity when all along the lines, it's about what God has created for you. You know, just because he may not look that way now, you know the story. He should look to see how she carries herself. He should look to see if this person basically is someone he wants to spend the rest of his life with her. Um, and that goes for someone who is secure with herself. Flippin it, a woman should look for a man who has integrity. A man who has desire to better himself. He has a vision and a plan. He's not craze or deranged. A man doesn't try to make her feel uncomfortable like pushing her into doing something like having sex or being intimate before she desires. Someone who shows he loves her and that he's really into her, he sticks to his word, and if he says he's gonna do something he does it. That he doesn't just disregard that. As far as a woman looking for something good; all the stuff is the opposite of what I'm saying. More on that, a woman looking at a man with no ambition, a woman looking at a man with no integrity, a woman looking at a man that doesn't do what he says he's gone do like if he says he's going to pick her up. A man who doesn't stand by his integrity or show any compassion or just doesn't show he's into her but then tries to trick her into thinking it.

Bachelor #4 response: Some men look for women to complete them. Some men look for women to serve as a trophy. Some men look for women to compliment them. Me personally, you should look for a woman that is not going to compromise herself to make you happy. A woman that is confident with herself and her ability to make you happy. Someone that is willing to meet you 50/50. Someone that truly and honestly loves you for you, and not what you have and can offer them. Someone you can see yourself waking up with for the rest of your life. Don't date a selfish woman. Don't date a woman without ambition. Don't date women that think men are dogs. If you go to a restaurant and a woman absolutely refuses to leave the tip or put in any portion of the bill, don't date her. If a woman is not comfortable enough to let you see her in her natural state; that is without make up, without her hair done or whatever, don't date her. Don't date a woman who carries so much baggage that she don't have room for another pair of socks; meaning if a woman has so much going on that she can't bear to take on anything else, that's probably a woman you can do without. Don't date your mother. A lot of people say that they look for a woman to have similar qualities to their mother. I think that's a huge character flaw. Your mother is just that, your mother and most people, like most psychologists may disagree. You might want a woman that shares similar characteristics as your mother like my mother raised me by herself

Chapter One - *Are Men & Women Really Different?*

where she's extremely strong and independent I would love my wife to be extremely strong and independent; but I don't want my mother. Don't try to find somebody that is identical to your mother. Granted every person has similar characteristics but don't take it to that extreme. As for women, I'm a very 50/50 kind of man, so everything a man should look for in a woman, a woman should look for in a man. My carnal rule for dating is; if you have to change who you are to make someone happy, you don't need to be with them. I would say for a woman, don't date a man that wants you to change who you are. If he can't accept you for who you are, then he probably don't need to be with you, and you don't need to be with him. Don't date a man purely because he has money, or purely because he's good looking, or purely because he's hung like a horse, or purely because he has a nice body. Date a man because he is what you always envisioned your husband to be. He is the person that you want to wake up to every morning.

Bachelor #5 response: Women should look for honesty and sincerity in men. I think sincerity more so than anything because people can say something and they'll mean something different so I think its sincerity and respect. Look for employable and some drive. Women should be interested in what's driving me, than what I drive. What does the brother want to do with his life? Does he want to just hang out at 40 years old and his biggest ambition is just making sure he can make it down to the club on the weekend, or is he trying to get his mind and his finances right. Does he have his finances right not so that you can come in and reap the benefits, but just because this brother is working to get himself together? You should be looking for somebody who's trying to help you. Give you time to help you get your finances straight. You shouldn't be looking for somebody to step in and help you correct your finances. There's a big difference. Because if you're looking for somebody to correct your finances, are you looking for another father, or are you looking for somebody who's going to take you by the hands and make your decisions for you. Now when you get that situation of course you want to say it should be respectful; but he's adopted another child basically. Though with your children, you tell your children what to do, where to go, when not to go, who they can go with and what they can do while you're there. You're a grown woman, so why should you want a man with that much say so or control over you. So that's why you should find a man that's going to help you correct your situation or guide you through correcting your situation but you got to correct it on your own. Those are the basics. Somebody who's going to legitimately care for you. Somebody who's going to be sincere with you. Somebody who is working to improve himself daily because that's important, and somebody who's spiritual at least spiritually minded. I think those thing are interchangeable for men to women as well.

Chapter One - *Are Men & Women Really Different?*

I don't think any man wants a woman that's going to always rely on him for everything. I don't think a woman wants a man that doesn't have any ambition, or needs her for any and everything. Honey I need some shoes, can you loan me $50 bucks, or can you give me $100. Nobody should want to be in those types of situations. Grown people shouldn't live like that. She should be looking for a man or he should be looking for a woman that's employed or employable. Educated, because you gotta consider the woman that you're dating could possibly be the mother of your children, and if you're married and get a dumb woman pregnant, you got a 50/50 chance that you're gonna have a dumb kid. That's just how it is. You gotta find the best of a bad market. If the momma don't want to work, let's be honest, it's a good possibility that the kid doesn't want to work. If the daddy don't want to work and the kid spends a lot of time with the dad, he's going to develop those traits so you got to find the right ingredients.

Question 7: *What types of men/women are there, define them and do men really want to be with any of them?*

Bachelor #1 response: You got the wanna be pimps, wanna be players, the momma's boys, the church goin man, and the God fearin man. Women: The want to be playettes. You got the wanna be pimpettes, wanna be I'm playing games. You know, you got the wanna be church girls that's frontin. You know they put on that skirt stuff, they do their hallelujah's, and shout round the church on Sunday's but all during the week woooo. You get in them panties all you want. So basically, you know you got the category that want to be in a relationship. Then you got the ones that really want it, but are afraid of it so they basically tryin to play the same games men have played. That's about that. What's a Hoe: I got to think about that. A hoe is a woman if she gives you head, she will swallow. A bitch: is a woman that don't mind bedding you down but will talk smack afterwards, and will try to dog you out in the streets. A Freak: is a women that just likes to get their freak on. I'm talking they just like to have sex. They basically call you up and say "hey listen, I need this thang tuned up. Come changed this oil for me. Come do yo thang." And that's basically a freak. Anything goes with a freak. A man may want a freak, but he'll never marry one. A player: a player is a brother that want to be a pimp, but don't really know how to have the pimp mentality. You see the average brother if he really knew the definition of a pimp, he wouldn't call himself a pimp because a pimp will do whatever a hoe will do, so a brother wouldn't actually call himself a pimp. Now a player is one that's basically out there playing the game. Got a whole bunch of women, telling a lot of em that he loves em, suppose to be they man, but he truly isn't. The average female is falling for it because he's cute, got a nice ride, they just happy to be with

Chapter One - *Are Men & Women Really Different?*

him, or they're proud that they actually with him cause he's that kind of catch.

Bachelor #3 response: Um,

Bachelor #4 response: There are two kinds of people in this world. The people that make things happen and the people that watch things happen. Women are just that way. You have women that are go getters and the women that kind of lay on their back waiting for somebody to do something for them. A hoe is a person that allows herself to be taking advantage of for sexual reasons and only sexual reasons. A woman that has sex with a multitude of men. A woman that has sex so freely and openly that she has no boundaries, and no end. She's willing to do anything at anytime with anyone. A bitch is a female dog. I don't like that word, but I would guess it's someone that has a very strong personality, a very strong attitude, very opinionated. My type of person actually. I wouldn't define a woman as a bitch because to me that's a female dog. A freak is a woman that is willing to try anything. A woman that is in touch with her sexuality, a woman that is a sexplorer. Someone that's willing to explore things sexually and enjoy sex. A man wants one in the bed and at home, but not a 100% freak. Nobody wants a 100% freak. I'm sure every person has heard it before a man wants a freak in the bed, and a lady in the street. I think that's the truest statement I think I've ever heard as far as that goes. Every man wants a freak, even if he don't actually want it to be done to him per say; he wants to know that whenever he has a notion or he has a desire, the person that he's with is willing to at least give him his desires. He don't have to go elsewhere for them. A player is anyone, and I mean man or female, that has the ability to juggle several relationships successfully. A true player is a person that don't have to lie about it. They don't have to lie about what they're doing and who they're doing it with. They create that understanding from the door. This is who I am, this is what I do, take it or leave it. And that person still attracts a person, and people to be in their circle, to be on their team.

Bachelor #5 response: The one group that I will comment on and that I'm most familiar with is guys like myself. Guys that work, don't necessarily have master degrees, bachelor degrees, but they work good honest jobs. They trained hard to get into the job that they have. They studied to get to the jobs that they have, and they carry those jobs out with precision. They want good honest long-term relationships. They want to do what it takes to build those relationships, or shall I say take that lump of coal and shape it into that magnificent diamond that it can be; but aren't going to take a lot of bull to get there. Because we know that just like there's a ton of beautiful, intelligent, strong, dedicated worthy women out there, you got

Chapter One - *Are Men & Women Really Different?*

that group of women that are no good, that are treacherous and all that other stuff you run into to get there, and a lot of times that builds up scar tissue around your heart, and on your mind. You just get to a point where you're like, she'll be good for this, but she ain't good for that. So you start weeding people out and you get to a point where I know what I want, I just don't want that with you. It's not right, it's not wrong; it's just the way it is. I'm familiar with those types of brothers because I happen to be one of em. But a lot of other guys, you got the guys that just want to just live off of other people. I don't really know a lot of people like that. You got, hustlers, scam artists, but the group I can speak on is the group I just referred to. As for women, you have a plethora of women that really know what they want, then you have all those little sub groups. The groupies, hoochies, all those other things where they think they know what they want, or they even believe that's what they really want but unfortunately; when they get to a certain point, it ain't cool being a 40 year old groupie or hoochie, and now you trying to make that transition trying to be somebody's wife. Well nobody really want you because while you were out there in your hoochie stage, everybody pretty much done had you and ain't nobody trying to marry the town whore. And truth be told, yeah a man can go out and be a whore, the difference being, when he finally does settle down, in his time of being a whore, he's learned how to make love so now his love making skills are off the meter. So the woman that he finally meets, and settle down with is reaping the benefits of this. But, for the one that was the hoochie, the process is different because it's not that she's necessarily learned how to make love better, but she's gotten so far away from what love making is, that she never really even has a chance to find love. She's found sex, she's found good sex. She's found out the easiest way to get it on; but it doesn't always equate to being able to transfer that to the new man she's with because now here it is, when she's with this new man and he can't put it on her, she can't necessarily teach him how to. Because part of her mind has told her if he can't put it on her, she ain't gone waste her time with him. But all she had to do is take all that information she was using to compare him to; because that's what she's basically doing, she's comparing him to all of her past loves and lovers, and if she can take that and say okay, well here's what I'm working with, this is somebody I care for, see if you put the care before the sex, you have a totally different dynamic. Now you take the care and all these other people whose experiences you've had, and say well if he does this, if he does that; but see you don't want to teach, you want to be pleasured off the bat and he's suppose to know how to come do this, but he don't know you like that, and you're not opening yourself up to him. So you may never find love, you'll always find good sex, but you won't be opened to love. And with men, it's just the opposite, see we start out having sex, and then we eventually develop to where we want to fall in love. And when we get to the point

Chapter One - *Are Men & Women Really Different?*

where we've had all these other conquests, we realize that's all they were. We were wasting time but we've taken that time to perfect our craft. Now a hoe, basically fucks anybody for any reason for some kind of gain. She's not doing it because that's the person she wants to be with, but because there's some kind of financial attachment to it. She's gone get a bill paid, she's selling herself short. A bitch is someone where everything's is always wrong in her world. She's always uptight about something, she always wants to fight and argue about something. She creates things to be mad about. A freak is just somebody that's adventurous. Every man wants a freaky woman, depending on how she carries herself, and as long as she's not a slut about it. A slut is somebody that get's freaky with everybody. She just has no limits. As I said, you want a girl that's freaky to some aspect because when you are together, you can make almost any situation right. Something big brought into the equation. You can just enjoy each other; you can explore each other's mind, body and souls. You not scared to try new things. But when you talk about somebody who's slutty, you talk about somebody who's doing this with people she just meets and nobody wants a slut. You see sluts have what you call shelf life. Just like with foods, they're good for three days yeah, that's pretty much what a slut is. She's good for a party, cause when me and my boys know where to go to hit it off, she's gone serve us up right. A player is just somebody who just has himself. Who's proud of what he does. People that are extremist. He doesn't pretend with anybody. He doesn't like anybody special. He says "look we're having a good time together let's just enjoy the time together. I'm not trying to be your man; you're not trying to be my woman. You sleeping with somebody else. I'm not trying to lie to anybody." He's playing his cards right. A momma's boy is somebody who can't get out of his mother's shadow. His momma has to make all his decisions, but he's a grown man. 30 years old, he lives between his momma house and his girlfriend's house. When he gets to his girlfriend house his momma be on the phone saying you better leave my baby alone. Thirty years old, still driving his momma's car back and forth to work. Gotta drop momma off to work so he can use her car to go on dates.

Question 8: Men bonding with their homies, what's up with that?

Bachelor #1 response: Basically it's a front. They don't want their fellas to think they don got whipped by some female to where they on locked down. But behind closed doors, he calling a sister every night, or at her house when he's not round his boys, but he try to hang out with his boys on the regular so they won't think he's been whipped.

Chapter One - *Are Men & Women Really Different?*

Bachelor #2 response: That's one I probably can't give a good answer to. Um, I personally never been that way. I never put men over women. Uh, basically although I wasn't into sports so I didn't cry if we lost the big game. I didn't slam into the lockers, like other guys, cause I really don't drink or smoke. Um it seemed like that was mostly the thing they did when they got together. They pitched in on a bag of weed, or pitched in on a 40 or something to drink, or whatever. I wasn't into drinking after the next cat. Smoking weed, you know the weed was all slobbed up. I've always been drug free so to me, when they did get high, and acted silly and flipped out, I was like that's lame so that I never really could get with that. I have a few close friends. We get together, you know, most times when men get together, women may come up, but I feel that um, it's a lot different. Cause you can usually walk by a table full of women 80 percent of the conversation is about their relationship with men, and with men basically 20 percent about the conversation will be about their relationship with women and about 80 percent of their conversation will probably be of a sexual nature. So I think that's the big difference. We may kick it about sports. We may kick it about work. We may just kick it about you know, other things. Superficial things. Cause like I said, men don't take it there emotionally like women do. I feel that I've always said that fishing is kinda like men's therapy. That on the fishing creek that something's may come out that no other time they ever really come out, but you know again with society if you take it back to the childhood, the rearing of competition and things of that nature, mostly with women, you don't talk about having real feelings or what bothers you like the movie. The brothers you know kinda summed it up; where they were playing basketball, you know they talked a little bit about the woman and they shot hoops, and they shot each other down, you know cause that's the risk that you take I mean anytime that you say you love or you're gonna get married, brothers feel like they should talk you out of it. For women, when they say that they bout to get married, everybody all happy for em, and all joyous or whatever; but brothers, even though often times a brother gets upset if you mention he's about to get married, especially around some other women, seem like they be hating or whatever cause men aren't really, really sure until that moment they're up in front of the preacher. Up until that time, almost anything can turn their head. Women on the other hand, he can just about be a serial murderer, and almost sleep with their mother before they decide they gone call off the wedding, because once they put their mind to it, their mind is to it, and a man's mind is very rarely to it to that particular level so again, it's just showing the differences between them.

Bachelor #4 response: What do you mean, it's necessary. I mean, it happens a lot, I think sometimes men use one another to escape from estrogen. When we want to get away from females sometimes we need to

Chapter One - *Are Men & Women Really Different?*

be around a man so we can feel like a man. Sometimes a man needs to feed his own ego by feeling just like that of a man.

Bachelor #5 response: There has to be a time when you become a man, you put childish things away. If you're a man and your still running with the boys, maybe you need to slow it down and start taking stock in the fact that you are a man now and you have to balance things off. Because as a man, you have a job, you have family, you have children, you have responsibilities, and your boys shouldn't come involved with those other things. They should be part of them, but your wife shouldn't always come home and see your boys sitting up in her living room. Your kids shouldn't be wondering if you're going to be coming to their game, or if you're going to be hanging out with your boys. When you are a child, you do childish things, when you become a man, it's time to put childish things away and walk like a man.

Question 9: What are some affective communication techniques both sexes should know?

Bachelor #1 response: Being honest, keeping it real. That would be the best communication. Say what you mean, mean what you say, so basically talking. A woman should be upfront right from the giddyup. Cause the average person know exactly what they want within 10-15 minutes into a relationships or conversation; I should say, not a relationship. The average woman know within 15-20 minutes whether or not she want to give the man some. She knows within the first 15 minutes whether he's relationship material or not. Whether she's feeling him on that level. She knows this, but the average person won't just come out and ask. You know where we heading with this? And the average female feel if they don't play the game they go lose it right away and it's hard to lose something you ain't got yet.

Question 10: How should a woman express she's not happy to a man?

Bachelor #1 response: Tell him, whatever's troubling her; she needs to just tell him. In all honesty, and I know this sounds childish, but sometimes a woman should write a letter and sit down and give it to him and let him read it and then wait for a response after the fact, that way she ain't got to say nothing and than if he don't respond in the right way, it's time for her to just step off.

Chapter One - *Are Men & Women Really Different?*

Question 11: *What's wrong with dating women in the new millennium compared to other generations?*

Bachelor #1 response: The new millennium woman is more independent and I think she's really intimidating to the average man. You know a brother wants to feel he's in control of every aspect of the relationship; financially, physically, mentally, and spiritually so if he's not, he's intimidated. And I think that's what's wrong with the new millennium type woman. She's independent, she can basically handle her own business, and the average brother figure if she can handle her own business, what I need to start a business with her, so the average brother won't. There's really nothing wrong with it, but I think the average woman today want both worlds. They want their independence; but yet they still want brothers to open the doors for em, take em out to dinner, and yet they quick to tell you they can handle their own. A woman has to be able to relinquish control and the average person can't because once you've been by yourself for such a long time, and the average woman that basically has a career and handling her own business, she's been by herself for so long, she's set in her ways and it's hard for her to relinquish some of that control, and the average brother is trying to get it, but he can't because she's quick to say "I don't need you to do nothing for me cause I can do it for myself."

Bachelor #4 response: Seeing that I'm only 24 and I haven't been through too many generations, so I'm only going on my perceptions and what I'm seeing. I think the new age woman; the new millennium woman is more concerned with her own personal gain, and with her own self being. Back in the day, you had women that were very comfortable with being at home, being moms, and allowing a man by definition I guess, to take care of them. I think the new millennium woman wants to take care of herself but know that a man is able to take care of her, at least a real woman. Then you have the other breed of woman that most women nowadays represent. They only want a man that have. I think back in the day, a woman was more susceptible to deal with a guy that made her happy if he had the potential to maybe one day bring something to the table. A woman now wants you to have everything that they ever wanted before they really decide to get with you.

Bachelor #5 response: Besides for their smart ass mouths, in past generations, you had women that were dedicated to their children, to their families, and had a sense of hope. They had a sense of hope that they were going to find their husbands, and have their children with their husbands. You had a sense of women wanting their children to be the best and the brightest and now you have a plethora of blended families where men are meeting women that already have a ton of kids and they don't have no

Chapter One - *Are Men & Women Really Different?*

control of the kids. Then you have the men that are coming into the situation where they already have 3 kids, dating somebody that has 3 kids and you have absolute chaos. Because a lot of times, that woman didn't have an established relationship with the kid's father. One of the fathers still want to come by every now and then and get his thing wet, and that was fine up until she met this new guy, and now there's conflict there and most men don't really like conflict. You have some that because they don't have nothing else going on in their lives don't mind getting in a nice scrap every now and then, but men that have stuff going on in their lives, generally don't want to do that, and I think overall there's a general sense of hopelessness. I think now you have women that are just willing to accept anything and consider it their fate rather than take the bull by the horn and make some serious hard decisions on what their willing to accept and what they're willing to throw out as trash and until that happens, there's always going to be that apathetic "what can I do about it, I can't change it," that whole thing about accepting whatever comes their way. They were going to keep spiraling down hill and can't afford to go any further down, because now, it's not about bettering themselves, it's about finding a baller. It's evident in our music. We got a woman right now talking bout she want a soldier. She needs a soldier. The problem I got with that is she grew up in the suburbs of Houston. So the music she's singing is going out to these urban areas where these young ladies are embracing it, because you got this beautiful talented singer telling her she needs a soldier, who ain't scared to ride out for her, who ain't scared to take a bullet for her, so now these young ladies are hearing this foolishness. The young men are hearing this foolishness so now they want to be a soldier who ain't scared to ride out for his down ass chick, or for his thug misses, and now he runs out, he got to keep his heart right and his chest all pumped out and you got these fools out here killing each other over nothing because they want to be the thug. They better get real, that ain't what's happening. If you want to stay on the bottom, that's the quickest way to do it, but all the folks that's singing this mess is at the top. They not scrappin for crumbs. She didn't get there by missing class, or missing voice lessons. Her boyfriend didn't get there by not practicing, not doing everything he could to stay dedicated to his cause, but we believe that somehow, we can all have these miraculous lifestyles by not doing the work and that's not gone happen. That's that sense of hopelessness.

Question 12: Independent, self sufficient, great gook, great mom, great sex so what's wrong with that?

Bachelor #4 response: I don't think there's necessarily anything wrong with that. That sounds like perfection.

Chapter One - *Are Men & Women Really Different?*

Bachelor #5 response: What's missing, there's nothing wrong with that, but what's missing is great communicator, great wife potential and a great wife does not mean she has great sex or she's a great cook but what about financially astute? What about willing to compromise, willing to take charge when necessary, or willing to back down when necessary? Sometimes those things are extremely important. Then there's a time when either person in the relationship has to step up, but there's also the time when somebody needs to recognize this ain't the time. Or maybe I should not coward down, but I should pick and choose my battles and this ain't the time.

Question 13: Do men like to be rescuers? (Damsel in distress)

Bachelor #1 response: The old man yes, the new man no. The old man was you know, he wanted to be that "I'm a rescuer." I'm gone be that knight in shining armor. I'ma save her. I'ma help her out with this. I'ma help pay her bills. I'm do this, thus, and that for her. The new brothers, like oh no. She can rescue me. She can spend her paper on me. She can buy me a car, let me drive around in her car, let me live in her apartment, and let me spend her money. Now is that being a punk, not necessarily. It's basically trying to be a player on the down low. He figures if she want to be a big baler, let her.

Bachelor #2 response: The damsel in distress mode, the hero. The bottom line is, that society says part of a man's role is not only to provide for her, but to protect her where she's broken. He pulls up and he changes her flat tire.

Bachelor #4 response: Yeah. Anything that feeds the ego a man likes to do. If they can feel like they're being a man by coming to the rescue of a woman and providing for her, then by all means, they're gonna do it. Cause that's like hitting a home run or scoring a touchdown. That's like bragging rights. I don't think most men go about it in the proper fashion, but that's something every man wants to be is a rescuer. Hell I love being a rescuer. I mean if you do something for somebody as far as being a rescuer, your pleasure and joy should come from doing something for someone else. Not the ability to throw something back in their face or what have you. I think most men nowadays do things just so they can hold something over a woman's head. Have leverage over them, like a bargaining chip almost, and I think that's not the proper fashion. The proper fashion would be to do it for the whole entirety of doing something for someone else.

Chapter One - *Are Men & Women Really Different?*

Bachelor #5 response: Some. I think real men step in. They see a problem, and they fix the problem. I think the guy that looks for the damsel in distress or always trying to be that rescuer, may have some issues. If that's what he gets his charge from, he's probably one of those guys that looks for women that makes a lot more money than him. He works at Xerox and she works at Wendy's because he knows they gone always need him. That's scary. But if your woman is in trouble, you should be there beyond a shadow of a doubt. But your woman shouldn't always be in trouble.

Question 14: Body talk, do men really try to interpret things this way?

Bachelor #1 response: Body language, yes. Cause the average woman, she know what she be doin. You know they thow a little extra twist on it, and they thow a little cleavage out there so basically they know what they gone do. And the average brother is basically reading their body language. The same thing with the sistas because they know exactly what a brothers all about within the first 15-30 minutes. They know exactly what's gone take place on the date. They know all this because it's already basically predetermined. Before you even pick each other up. And the average brother can tell when he goes to pick a woman up for a date based on what's she's got on what's gone go on that night. Say for instance, if you're invited over to the house for a movie or something, and she has on a sweat suit. It's on, cause it's easy accessible. Easy in and easy out. If somebody is upstairs, oops just pull em right back up. But if you wear some tight jeans, that's hard to get out of. But a sweat suit, the first thing you say is "well I'm home, I just want to be comfortable" you be like yeah a'ight, no problem. Same thang with a skirt cause half of em don't do nothing but have on a thong underneath. And with a skirt, you don't truly half to take it off, you just pull it up, smack it up, then flip it, you can rub it down if you wanna.

Bachelor #4 response: Of course. Everything has a reason and has a purpose. I think most men look for a woman to do something or show them some sign of interest that is read solely on body talk unless they're just bold and say I'ma just go over there and holla. Most dudes look for something to go on and that's for everything. If they decide they want to go in for the kiss, they look for a sign through the body language of the woman to see if that's a good or bad move. Same thing with sex. If I think I can try to have sex with her tonight, and she's not going to try to kill me or if she might even be willing, I'm going to determine that based on her actions and her body talk over the course of our previous date or telephone conversation or what have you.

Chapter One - *Are Men & Women Really Different?*

Bachelor #5 response: Sometimes, it can be real overt and then sometimes it can be just very obvious. They say that there's certain signs that a let's you know that a woman is interested in you. If you're sitting across from a woman and she crosses her leg and the foot that she has dangling is pointed in your direction, that's suppose to be a sign that she's attracted to you. If you're sitting next to her and she's leaning towards you, it's supposed to be a sign that she's interested. If she's leaning away from you that mean that she's ready for whatever. But if she's sitting and she has her foot pointed toward you, that's supposed to mean like come hither. But a lot of times, it could just be her natural mannerism, and it might not have anything to do with you. But a man being a man, he just have to go ahead and take that plunge. What's the worst that could happen, she could tell you no. A woman flipping her hair naturally she's flirting. Until she starts taking off clothes, there are no definite signs. Until the clothes actually come off, you're still guessing.

Question 15: Define Love?

Bachelor #1 response: I honestly don't know what love is. Me personally, I thought I did, but I don't. Right now, nothing has moved me, no woman that I have ever met have moved me to where I can say the earth stopped. Where my heart stopped and skipped a few beats. I think my marriages were basically an infatuation. I think it was a fantasy of what I thought a marriage should be. What I thought a relationship should be, based on what I grew up around, what I saw. Based on my grandparents, my parents, I think that's what I had envisioned in my mind. What it should be. Get a certain age, get married, have kids, boom. And live happily ever after. Truly what love is right now, I really don't know.

Bachelor #4 response: Love is not a definable word in my vocabulary. Love is not a word it's a feeling. And you can not define a feeling. Love is something to experience; it's not something to explain.

Bachelor #5 response: It's over rated. I really don't know how to define love. You have the Shakespearian type love, Romeo, Romeo, where for art thou? You got all that good old stuff romantic tragedy where you both kill each other because you can't have each other. Then you have the Hollywood romance or Hollywood love where they overcome all adversities, trials, and tribulations, and everything always ends happily ever after with the 3 kids the dog, and the house in the suburbs. See those don't necessarily equate to love. There was a situation where there was a couple I use to know, and I heard this information second hand, but the mother didn't like the husband. They ended up getting into a financial

Chapter One - *Are Men & Women Really Different?*

situation and lost their home. They left where they were living, came back to Rochester and gonna stay with the mother. The mother said, the daughter and the kids could stay in her home, but her husband couldn't stay there. She told her mother the children can stay in the home, but if my husband isn't welcomed in your home, my place is with my husband and they proceeded to sleep in the car that night. Whatever the situation was, she stood by her husband. Which is what a good wife does. That's love. That's love and respect and that's the type of relationship I want. Where it's not about how people perceive what you do, but your thoughts are always how you can look out for me and my family and my thoughts are always how I can look out for you and my family.

Question 16: What do you truly want in a mate/wife?

Bachelor #1 response: I can't answer that question honestly either cause I'm not truly looking right now, and if I was, I'd say she'd have to be a God fearing woman. Able to be submissive, not necessarily somebody that's gonna be a robot, but submissive, in other words, know that I'm a man, but be able to say you know, this is a God fearing man. I know God is leading, and guiding my spouse to make the right decisions based on this family and she's able to trust me on that level.

Bachelor #4 response: Confidence, ambitious, a cook, I'm sorry to be a little superficial, but I would like her to be pretty. A self-starter, a self-motivator, and a woman that is willing to give herself to me wholly. A woman that is confident in herself and her ability to make me happy. A woman that wants me in the same regard that I want her. I don't want her to feel like she's settling, and I don't want to feel like I'm settling. As far as dating, I really don't date anymore. I'm looking for a wife. I guess I do date but yes, right now, I date according to what I'm looking for in a wife because that's what I want right now.

Bachelor #5 response: Basically, I'm looking for someone whose absolutely selfless and committed to our relationship. She's about the business of us being and staying together. Committed to me, respects me, loves me and all of my flaws. My beautiful perfect flaws.

Question 17: Does Mrs. Right really exist?

Bachelor #1 response: I'd say yes.

Bachelor #4 response: I believe so. Mrs. Right, Ms. Almost Right, Ms. Right now. Ms. Right now is the woman that I may not be exactly what I'm looking for, but she makes me content. She fulfills the majority of my

Chapter One - *Are Men & Women Really Different?*

necessity. She's not somebody I can see myself spending the rest of my life with, but I can definitely see her sticking around for a while. You can never know if they'll be the person to stick around long, but usually that's the person that usually gets me in trouble. I have a friend now that is Ms. Right now. She's a wonderful person. I'm happy when I'm with her, but I can't see myself spending the rest of my life with her because she has a tough old flaws in her characteristic that I can't see myself dealing with for the rest of my life, but its okay for right now because it's temporary.

Bachelor #5 response: Somewhere. She exists somewhere, even if it's in the bottom of a test tube. Maybe even if I have to find it in a blow up doll, but the blow up doll you can't teach 'em how to cook, but I won't rule out the test tube theory. I think she does exist, I think it's just a matter of finding the person that loves you, respects you, will cherish you, just like you'll cherish, love, and respect them, and be willing to compromise, and find those common areas where we're building constantly, consistently toward our future.

Question 18: Commitment, what does that mean to you

Bachelor #1 response: I don't know. Haven't been there yet. Commitment basically is two people that's willing to commit to each other spiritually, mentally as well as physically at every level there is to mention. You know being open, honest with someone. Uh basically like I said tryin to take that thang to a level of possible, possible marriage.

Bachelor #4 response: Giving yourself to someone holistically and only to them. Being loyal to a person. Being truthful to a person. Allowing a person into your life, into your thoughts.

Bachelor #5 response: Means everything. I think that's one of the things that's lacking in relationships. People don't really understand what it takes to be committed. You have to be dedicated to your cause. You have to say this is the person that I want to spend the rest of my life with, then why are you only giving it five years? Why are you only giving it a few months? Or maybe your prep work was wrong. Maybe you based your marriage on the wrong thing. Commitment means you're doing any and everything to promote your marriage and your relationship. You're dedicated to your family, your kids, your spouse, whatever it takes to get you all to that next level. I think people need to go ahead and decide if they make the commitment to be married, that they gone go ahead and stick it out because it's not gone be easy. It's not gone be a piece of cake. It's not gonna be just everything is always gone go right. They got to decide that the weather is going to be bad some days, and stick it out. The weather is

Chapter One - *Are Men & Women Really Different?*

gone be good some days, but they stick it out. On your job, you put up with a lot of stuff that you don't want to put up with. You go through union contracts that don't go through, you get over looked for promotions, people stay on the job for 30 years and they've had all these negative experiences, but they've always stayed. They stayed and at the end of the road, they finally got that pension, after all that shit they took on that job; but you gave your marriage 5 years? But your marriage produced beautiful kids. It had the potential to blossom into something fantastic, but you gave your marriage 5 years. You gave your corporation 30. What did your marriage do that your job didn't do to you? We get things twisted up, and part of that commitment needs to be to your overall financial future. You're overall financial future together. If you're not looking down and saying where I want to be in 30, 40, 50 years, something's wrong. Maybe one of ya'll not as dedicated as the other. Because if you look down and say in 5 years I want to be in Cancun, in Hawaii, what do you want to be doing with your husband or your wife in 45 years? Have ya'll even talked about the grandkids graduations, maybe even playing with the great grand kids. Those things need to be discussed. Because those things are the things that are going to keep you focused and committed to each other cause you're looking at the overall strength and unity of your commitment.

Question 19: Why are you single?

Bachelor #1 response: I choose to be single at this present time due to the fact that I want to be able to find myself. In other words, I honestly felt in my first two marriages, I was half a man and I attracted half a woman. In other words, it equaled to half a marriage. Now I'm trying to make myself a whole man, putting God first in everything that I do. Becoming a whole man that way I can attract a whole woman. That way I'll have a whole marriage. Cause basically one plus one equals one in God's sight. Can you feel me?

Bachelor #4 response: Mrs. Right now is just that. I found the person that I thought to be Mrs. Right but she didn't feel the way I felt about her I don't think and because of that, I wouldn't allow her to settle. Like I said speaking of the new millennium woman, she's a wonderful woman. She's everything I ever wanted in a woman; her only issue with me is that I don't have everything that she wants me to have right now. I drive rented cars mostly, and she wants me to own a car. I rent she wants me to have a house, that sort of thing. Even though she's my age, she's just starting her career, I looked forward to building a life with her, but she wants to come into a life that's already built. She's deals with two other gentlemen right now, one is a drug dealer and he has a whole lot of money. She deals with

Chapter One - *Are Men & Women Really Different?*

him solely because he has money and he's able to provide for her. The other gentleman she's actually in love with is in the music industry. He's a music producer. He also has money, but he has no time for her because he's always on the road. He'll send for her to come to NY for a week, she'll see him the day she gets there and the next month he'll get up and leave and be on a plane and he'll come back the night before she leaves. She basically put it to me like, I'm interested in you, I have an interest and I love you, and I wouldn't mind being with you, but my heart is with this person and my time is with this person.

Bachelor #5 response: I don't really know. I was in a relationship for quite a long time and I thought that I wanted the person to be my wife and as luck would have it, turns out that's not the way things work. I spent a lot of time trying to make that situation work out and I'm sure she did too, we were both very patient. Trying to be there through a lot of situations and circumstances, and it turned out that we'd be together for a while. We'd break up, we'd date other people, I'd date other people, and we'd get back together and even drop other people to get back together with each other. Just relationships that were going well just walked away from because I really thought that was supposed to be my future. When I finally realized that things were over, I walked away and spent a weekend with a woman and that was something I normally wouldn't have done, but when I did that, I knew that I had to be out of that other relationship because I spent the entire weekend with this woman with no regard, no thought of consequence for what I had done, or what I was doing, and at that point I knew that I didn't have a future with that person because things had finally gotten to a point where it was time to say goodbye. So right now, I'm just laying back, enjoying the fact that I'm single and all that it entails, so ladies, ya'll pick this up, and um, holla at me. Holla at yah boy!

Question 20: *Why do you think women are single?*

Bachelor #1 response: Same thing I said earlier. I think women are single due to the fact that the average man is intimidated. He feels that there's nothing he can do for her that she can't do for herself. So basically, they want to be in a relationship but the average brother is not stepping to them like that and I think it's based on intimidation.

Bachelor #4 response: I think any real woman can have a man if she so please. Any woman to me that is by herself is either not willing to look for Mr. Right or don't want to look. By look I don't mean literally look. I don't mean go out on a manhunt. I mean more so be open to the idea of being in a serious relationship.

Chapter One - *Are Men & Women Really Different?*

Bachelor #5 response: Different women, different reasons. That's kinda hard to gauge cause some; I really respect the women that have sworn off dating for the sole purpose of being good mothers to their children. And you do have some that that is absolutely, unequivocally, the only reason that they are not dating. They make the conscious decision, I want to take some time and just bond and be with my children. I got to work all day; I can at least give this time to my children and help them be much better and more focus individuals. And there are some women who are single just becauseit happens that way. Maybe because they aren't meeting the right type of people, or they are not the right type of person that people want to meet. Lately I hear a lot of women saying that men are intimidated by them because they are independent black women. And largely, I think that's just bull. I think in a lot of those cases, those women tend to be very abrasive. And abrasive does not reflect strength. See strength is reflected in having the power and choosing not to use it, that's strength and being abrasive is assuming you have the power and you're constantly trying to make people know that you have the power. It's a huge difference because people respect powerful people that are humble. But nobody respects the bully and if you come in as a bully, people are repelled by you being a bully. They're not attracted to the bully, they're attracted to the person that carries themselves well, and knows that at any given minute, I'm running this show. I'm always running the show, but I don't have to prove it. That's the person that people want to be around. Because they know how things are going down and they allow things to go down. They don't have to sweat nobody. They don't have to make nobody bow down and coward down to them because they have internal strength, they have inner strength, and that's way above all things. They have class so a lot of those women interpret that as people being intimidated by them. No, it's not intimidation; they just don't like a loud, brash woman. Then you have some women that just are so focused on what they're doing, they just don't notice people that are attracted to them, because they're so focused on what they have to do. I think there are a ton of reasons why people are single, but I really feel the average sister that thinks that all men are intimidated by them think that because it ain't like that. You can be very intelligent, you can have college degrees, you can make great money, and it's a lot of sisters like that. But it's a lot of the sisters that you hear them way before you see them, or you hear about them way before you meet them. Good brothers really don't like them because they're just obnoxious.

Chapter One - *Are Men & Women Really Different?*

Question 21: Why do you think men are single?

Bachelor #1 response: Men choose to be single cause it's a black man's buffet out there right now sista. Brothers feel they got the pick of the litter so why tie down with one. They can have one on the side, one over here, one over there and everybody don't care what's going down as long as they being treated right at the specific time when it's they time. Can you feel me?

Bachelor #4 response: Because they want to have their cake and eat it too. They want the ability to say they have someone that they can call their own, but be free to go do whatever they may choose to do.

Bachelor #5 response: That has more answers than the first questions. Largely for the same reason as women. You have a harder time finding a good caliber of women you want to be with. A woman you want to help you raise your kids, who wants to be there to nurture your children.

Question 22: What will you tell your young adult children about dating (13-18 years old)?

Bachelor #4 response: I think I'm just going to give them the basics. I'm gonna tell them not to give themselves completely to a woman without knowing what her intent is, but I think dating is something that you have to learn from your experiences. I think experience is the best teacher in that regard because like I said every relationship is different so I can't tell them what worked and didn't work for me cause that may have absolutely no bearing on the people that they may deal with. Because the women that my father was dating is not the same woman that I'm dating, and the things that worked for him to get my mother wouldn't work for me to find my wife. I don't think the things that work for me right now is going to work for my son, so I wouldn't necessarily tell him anything. I will more or less be there for moral support, or what have you, and allow him to experience it for himself.

Bachelor #5 response: Be careful. I've already started talking to my kid about dating. The thing I told her, the most important thing I told her is if you date or you hanging out and he doesn't want to meet your family, that's the boy you want to get away from. Because he doesn't have your best interest at heart. If he doesn't want to be around your family or doesn't want to know your family, or doesn't want your family to know him that means there's something in him that he knows aren't right. One he doesn't measure up, and two that means he got some shady plans for you. You should get away from him as quickly as possible. Don't carry

Chapter One - *Are Men & Women Really Different?*

yourself as a tramp. One of the first lessons I told my daughter before she started dating, we went to the store, I went one way; she went another, and she came up and went grabbing on my arm "ooh daddy, ooh, ooh ," and I told her I said, you don't have to act like a whore. If there's something you want, ask me. If I'm going to buy it, my answer is always yes or no. You don't have to sell yourself like that. Whores carry themselves like that. You're not a whore. Ever since that day, if my daughter wants something, she asks for it and my answer is still yes or no. I put it to her that way because I wanted her to understand, you don't sell yourself to men to get what you want.

DELBRA BARR
CHAPTER ONE: ARE MEN AND WOMEN REALLY DIFFERENT
REFLECTION
THAT WAS THEN (2004)

ABOUT WOMEN

According to the bachelors, there are some things about men and women that we have to just learn how to "accept" and not try to understand about our differences and how we think and respond to things in life. I've come to understand that there are somethings that just make up our psyche or who we are as human beings and once we learn how to understand those differences, we can communicate differently. I'm not saying we need to agree with everyone, but if we're looking to establish a healthy relationship with others, we need to understand there are some things that define who we are as men and women and we have to understand those differences. Like how women are more emotional and nurturing. It's hard for women to turn off these emotions. I'm not saying it's impossible, just hard. Women have come to believe if they say "no," then they'll be missing out on what could be great relationships, but in the words of one of the bachelors, "you can't miss out on what you never had," and if you tell him no and he leaves, then he never was "mister right." In reflecting on my own personal relationships, I have settled many times for dating a man even though I could tell his foundation was a little "shaky." Instead of setting boundaries, I went along by saying "ok" because I didn't want them to think I was trying to judge them by questioning the issues I saw or by telling them no. I thought if I put my foot down too early in the "relationship," then I would be missing out on the opportunity to see if he was in fact Mister Right. Unfortunately, in most cases, he always turned out to be Mister Wrong anyway.

ABOUT MEN

I learned that men really care about their "ego" and they recognize how much it influences their perception about dating and relationships. A man's ego will stop him from dating her if he feels she's dating either too many men or she's dating someone he knew. Men like to feed their ego by feeling like she's learning from him. That he's her first in something and that he can conquer something, and if he can't feel like that, then he can't be serious about her. I've learned that men really are looking for a woman who shows she has morals and values and when she doesn't then he's game to take the ride, but he knows he'll be getting off. No matter what she tries to do to keep him, he knows he'll be moving on to another one. A man is like a kid. They'll keep on trying you to see if you let him get away with it. If you do, then cool, but once you do, he'll never consider you as a serious candidate to take home to momma. One of the bachelors shared you can tell that a man's not serious with you because he'll go to all of your company parties, even some of your family gatherings, but he'll never ask you to come over his parents house or to his functions. You're good enough for him to go to your functions, but

DELBRA BARR
CHAPTER ONE: ARE MEN AND WOMEN REALLY DIFFERENT
REFLECTION - *continued*
THAT WAS THEN (2004)

not for him to take you to his. A man won't let you into his world or his heart unless he's serious about you and when he is, you'll know it because he'll tell you and he'll back it by showing you. He'll do what he says he's going to do. If you're still wondering if he is serious with you or if he's taking your relationship seriously, if he doesn't make keep his promises, then trust me, he ain't! He'll let you be "Ms. Right Now," knowing that you're not "Mrs. Right." He won't commit to anything. He'll make you think he's committing to what you're saying without him actually saying it. Take for instance, you ask him what type of relationship you guys have and he says he's just "chillin, taking it one day at a time." Trust me, that's all he is going to be doing with you. You'll be in a "relationship" all by yourself. Some men believe there are two types of relationships. The wife and everybody else. Women however need to know what type of relationship it is: Are you platonic friends, booty call or get busy friends? Are you dating or in a committed relationship where you are only intimate with each other while you're working on "building or establishing" something more? Are you engaged or are you married? Some men won't commit to any of these because they don't believe in them. You either are, or you aren't. Now there are some men who believe there are different levels in relationships; but there are more men who don't than who do.

MRS DEBBIE CAKES
CHAPTER ONE: ARE MEN AND WOMEN REALLY DIFFERENT
REFLECTION
THIS IS NOW (2017)

The true difference between men and women is that men take the time to study women and gain an understanding of her psychological, emotional, and behavioral makeup so they can map out their game plan for how they will treat her; and women on the other hand never knew they should do the same. Society spends a great deal of time teaching women how to raise their children, and even express the need for her to look good; but women are never told that to establish a long lasting relationship she needs to learn how to study men and make them "prove" they are worthy to receive her heart before she entertains the thought of being intimate with him. Men love "Sexplorers." You know, women who are game to try anything sexually, but to a man, in the end, instead of securing a long lasting relationship, she'll find herself getting a reputation because men love to brag about their conquests. Many years ago, I was in the grocery store with my daughter and as we got ready to check out, I saw one of my exes. We said hello, and I introduced him to my daughter. He remembered her because she was a child when we dated, but she didn't remember him. As we were talking, he turned to my daughter and tells her "you know I could've been yo daddy!" This same scenario happened to me on at least three separate occasions and it shocked me that they felt the need to do that because my child didn't need to know my intimate partners were. When people do things like this, we have to learn how to ourselves what the hidden message to their action was really all about. What he was really saying was, "man; I let this one get away." Yet, instead of acknowledging that fact, he felt the need to share something that made him feel good about himself; even if it made me look bad. This scenario also happened to my mother with a guy she knew from her past. I tell you ladies, if you really want to learn how to understand men, read my book *"If I Can't Be The Cake, I Won't Be The Crumz."* However; in the meantime, these are something's you will need to be willing to do if you want to secure a long lasting monogamous, heterosexual relationship.

1. Learn how to set boundaries against the things that make you uncomfortable.
2. Stop feeling like he will lose interest if you start asking questions too soon.
3. Stop feeling like you will be a failure if the relationship does not last. Start seeing it as you can't afford to keep wasting time trying to establish something when you are the only person doing the work.
4. Start learning how to accept his truth as his truth. Many times a person tells you their truth, but it's so harsh you tell yourself he can't possibly mean what he's said. The truth is the truth and as the old saying goes "The truth will set you free."
5. If you have children, stop putting your needs before them. They did not ask to come into this world; therefore they deserve for you to give them the chance to grow up in a home where they are loved, nurtured and protected.
6. Stop settling for crumz. You will never get full, and you will always keep wanting more!

CHAPTER ONE: ARE MEN AND WOMEN REALLY DIFFERENT
MY FAVORITE QUOTES

The My Favorite Quote section is where I will identify the comments that were made by the bachelors that really stuck out to me. They stuck out because I had never heard them, or I really was taken by surprise when the men shared this as their "truth."

He knows what he's doing, and he doesn't jeopardize himself or those around him for petty gain p.17

The game you trying to run on me, I taught them niggas how to run on you. p.18

What I realize is that often times; their greatest asset is their greatest popularity point which is their femininity. Men are not looking for competition; men are looking for someone that's complimentary. p.18

When something's bothering me, how do you read me, how do you relate to me? She makes me think it's my idea when it's her idea. p.18

As we grow up, we eventually want the same thing. p.19

So I fake like I love you to get the lust I want. Women are taught to give him the lust he wants to get the intimacy she want. See we have to exchange that love for lust. p.19

Men naturally are conquerors. Women are nesters which mean they want to set up homes, have and raise children, and be family oriented. Men want to have a nice comfortable place to call home, but we need to have our wandering space. Women don't understand that. p.19

Women should know that we're only going to do what you let us do. p.21

Men, don't always want what they ask for. Because we ask you to do a three way, maybe you shouldn't do it. Because maybe, that's not what we really want you to do. p.21

Always let 'em go in their pocket first before you go in yours p.22

Never give a woman everything. Always leave her wanting something. p23

If you do nice things for her, and she has to think about whether she should do nice things for you, then she 'bout don't respect you. p. 23

A man who doesn't stand by his integrity or show any compassion or just doesn't show he's into her but then tries to trick her into thinking it p.25

CHAPTER ONE: ARE MEN AND WOMEN REALLY DIFFERENT
MY FAVORITE QUOTES - *continued*

You should look for a woman that is not going to compromise herself to make you happy p. 25

Don't date a woman who carries so much baggage that she don't have room for another pair of socks p.25

A woman should look for a man who has integrity. A man who has desire to better himself. He has a vision and a plan. p. 26

Women should be interested in what's driving me, than what I drive. p.26

She should be looking for a man or he should be looking for a woman that's employed or employable. p.27

If the daddy don't want to work and the kid spends a lot of time with the dad, he's going to develop those traits so you got to find the right ingredients. p.27

You get to a point where I know what I want, I just don't want that with you. p.29

We start out having sex, and then we eventually develop to where we want to fall in love. p.29

Thirty years old, still driving his momma's car back and forth to work. Gotta drop momma off to work so he can use her car to go on dates. p.30

He can just about be a serial murderer, and almost sleep with their mother before they decide they gone call off the wedding, because once they put their mind to it, their mind is to it. p.31

If you're a man and your still running with the boys, maybe you need to slow it down and start taking stock in the fact that you are a man now and you have to balance things off. p.32

When you are a child, you do childish things, when you become a man, it's time to put childish things away and walk like a man. p.32

It's hard to lose something you ain't got yet. p.32

Now you have women that are just willing to accept anything and consider it their fate rather than take the bull by the horn and make some serious hard decisions on what their willing to accept and what they're willing to throw out as trash and until that happens p.34

CHAPTER ONE: ARE MEN AND WOMEN REALLY DIFFERENT
MY FAVORITE QUOTES - *continued*

The new brothers, like oh no. She can rescue me. She can spend her paper on me. She can buy me a car, let me drive around in her car, let me live in her apartment, and let me spend her money. p. 35

But a man being a man, he just have to go ahead and take that plunge. p.37

I think it was a fantasy of what I thought a marriage should be. What I thought a relationship should be, based on what I grew up around, what I saw. p.37

Mrs. Right, Ms. Almost Right, Ms. Right Now. Ms. Right now is the woman that I may not be exactly what I'm looking for, but she makes me content. p. 38

She exists somewhere, even if it's in the bottom of a test tube. p.39

People don't really understand what it takes to be committed. p.39

Your marriage produced beautiful kids. It had the potential to blossom into something fantastic, but you gave your marriage 5 years. You gave your corporation 30. What did your marriage do that your job didn't do to you? p. 40

I was half a man and I attracted half a woman. In other words, it equaled to half a marriage. p. 40

But nobody respects the bully and if you come in as a bully, people are repelled by you being a bully. p. 42

But it's a lot of the sisters that you hear them way before you see them, or you hear about them way before you meet them. p. 42

Brothers feel they got the pick of the litter so why tie down with one. p. 43

You don't sell yourself to men to get what you want. p. 43

KEEP | STOP | START

In my professional life as a Quality Engineer which is a Software Tester, I work with a team who are charged to ensure the design and implementation of software is sound based on the business requesting the work, and the customers who will be using the application. There is a methodology called Agile which encourages the team to implement efficient processes in order to achieve these goals, and at the end of the sprint or the designed project time frame, the team reflects on the implementation of their work and discuss what worked well, and what they are doing that should be changed. This same methodology works great in applying these principles in our everyday lives, so at the end of each section of the book, you will have the chance to reflect on what the bachelors have shared and use the pages provided to note what you will

KEEP DOING – Whatever you're doing, it is working so reflect on the behaviors you exhibit that keep you from falling victim to a man's predatory techniques when they try to talk to you.

START DOING – Based on their responses, what comments cause you to think about what you need to START DOING differently when it comes to communicating with men and others who think differently than you?

STOP DOING – Based on their responses, what do you need to STOP DOING when it comes to how you respond to men, and in your views and perspective about how they communicate to you?

Chapter One - *Are Men & Women Really Different?*

KEEP DOING

_____

_____

_____

_____

_____

_____

START DOING

_____

_____

_____

_____

_____

_____

STOP DOING

_____

_____

_____

_____

_____

_____

Question Two
Rules of Dating

Question Two
Rules of Dating

Exactly what comes to mind when you think about the word "dating?" Are you establishing a relationship with someone where both of your end goals would be to determine if that person is right for you and if they would be a great long term partner? Is it just an opportunity to spend time with someone to get to know them intimately? Is it just a way to "relate" with one another? A woman's views about dating is vastly different than a man's. The questions asked to the bachelors in this chapter were designed to get an understanding about what they thought about dating and establishing relationships. What do men really want? What questions should women be asking if her intention is to be taken seriously in their goal to establish her desire for a long lasting relationship? What does she need to adjust in her dating practice if that is her intention? Many times we based our requirements for relationships on worldly and fleshly desires. Do you want a partner and a friend, or someone who gives you amazing sex but that's all they have to give. Eventually you will find that sex is not enough to sustain a long lasting relationship. There has to be more but many times we don't know how to define what "more" is.

Because of the bachelors schedules, I either didn't get the opportunity to ask each of them every question, or the answers that were given by the bachelors I met with provided me great insight about what men thought so I was able to answer many of the unanswered questions. Your exercise going forward is to not only think about the questions I have identified, but to learn how to start asking pertinent questions to the men in your life to see what their thoughts and views are about things. Whenever you see the answer to a question is blank, take the time to begin your own investigative quest with the men in your life to see what their views are if they are in alignment with yours. This process will teach you not only how to start asking questions, but how to ask crafty and specific questions in order to get men to tell you the whole truth and not the partial truth. They say the truth will set you free, but there is another saying that in every lie there is some truth. Men have a way of telling you what you want to here and not the "truth," and that is because women don't ask men questions that force them to tell the whole truth and nothing but the truth. You have to learn how to be crafty and ask the right questions. You have to challenge men by getting in their heads, just like they get in ours.

Chapter Two – *Rules of Dating*

Question 23: What are some effective courting rituals/techniques?

Bachelor #1 response: Well, I can't answer that honestly, I'm not trying to court, I'm not tryin to date. But if I was, I'd basically have to sit down and think about it. It would be based on the woman that I met. You know what's she like, what she like to do, what's her turn on's, what's her turn off's, and it's very important a woman be honest when she's talking to an individual, that way he can know a little bit more about her. For instance, if we exchange phone numbers and decide to meet up for dinner, I'm go come geared up cause that's just how I roll. And based on what she wears to the dinner date, it gives me a little bit of a chance to understand what type of a person she is. Is she laid back, is she casual, is she gone be up front or what? At dinner we might conversate about what she does for a living, has she been married, is she in a relationship, why isn't she in a relationship, what happened during that relationship and the average woman might tell me it's none of your business which is cool; but that is telling me she might have something to hide. Because um, I honestly feel if you're not in a relationship if you give me a little bit of heads up why you not, and it could be things just didn't work out, but if you tell me it's none of my business, it's like you tryin to hide something from me and that's basically a turn off. But if it's going well and if I honestly feel that she's worth another date, I might let her call me in a couple days. But would I call her, definitely not, because if I call her it'll make me seem like I'm too eager to push toward a relationship and I don't want anybody to get the misinterpretation of me so they would have to give me a call. If she calls me the next day, I might give the brush off. Say I'm kinda busy, I got things going on right now, can you holla back at me later on this weekend or something. Regardless of the chemistry between the two of us, she'd have to take it there, not me. I'm not looking to be wooed. If I met her and her conversation is on point, then I might holla at her but it won't be the next day. No matter what. A few days have to go by before I call her back. If I called her back after them days and she honestly gave me the brush off, then I'd be like okay maybe she wasn't the one. And if she didn't, then I'd set up a dinner date, but on my turf.

Bachelor #4 response: Show and go as I like to call it. When you flash a little cash to get them to go with you. I don't know. I have a very unique method I'd like to think. I don't chase, I'm a natural flirt so I flirt with everyone not so much for dating purposes but I like to see people smile. But I know when I'm looking for someone to date. If I'm at a club, bar, or restaurant and I make eye contact with someone, and I feel that there is an interest there based on as we spoke about earlier "the body talk," then I may approach them more so on the level of just hi how are you doing. Is it

Chapter Two – *Rules of Dating*

a possibility I can get to know you at a later date? Some people take a more direct approach.

Bachelor #5 response: For men, on the first date, don't ask her to pay for the meal. Women on the first date don't order stuff that you can't pronounce. Don't order stuff that you wouldn't normally order if you went out with your girlfriends. Men, remember you were asking this woman out because it's was somebody you were interested in, you were attracted to, so you should treat them like you're interested and attracted to them. Maybe show up with a rose, open the door for them when you get ready to let them into the car. And fellas take your car. Drive a car on the date, or at least pay for a cab but you shouldn't be relying on her to provide you transportation for the date because you will be asking her for some booty; and if she had to provide for the dinner, the transportation, the tip, what was your purpose for being there. She could've done all that on her own, I'm sure she wasn't that hard up for company. I'm sure. So for the dudes, it would be a brother to make sure he can afford the date, do a little planning, do a little pre thinking. Some don'ts, don't get drunk, don't sit there and chain smoke especially if your girl is not a smoker. Women, don't waste our money. If we're paying for a date to take you out to eat, eat and enjoy your meal. Don't order dinner and dessert and take ¾ of the food home, planning for your lunch for tomorrow. Sit there and eat. Order a piece of cake for tonight and one for your baby. What's that all about? And then volunteer sometimes to pay the tip; if he pays the bill, why don't you volunteer to pay the tip? Show him that you're interested in him. If he opens the door and holds the door for you, reach across and unlock the door. Or you know what, while you're in the car, try to find where the power lock is, surprise him, even if he has remote entry. Why don't you just reach across and open the door. It's not going to hurt you? All it's going to do is give you more cool points. Don't sit there and complain about everything, "It's sho'll moving slow" and "It's a 1,000 people in the restaurant." Sometimes just be a little bit more mellow. And brothers need to not get so uptight about things too. Take things in stride and don't always expect to have sex on the first date just because you take a girl out. That's a turn off to women. From the time they get in the car, you talking about what we gone do when we get back to yo place, this that and the other. It's not that they don't want to do it; they don't want to be pressured into it.

Chapter Two – *Rules of Dating*

Question 24: Is it Love or Lust at first site?

Bachelor #1 response: Could be a little bit of both. I honestly don't believe in love at first site. But that's just me personally. I honestly believe in order for you to love somebody you got to get to know them, talk to them a little bit, but to see em, that's really lust. Big booty, big titties, you know how that go. You see a brother with a nice chest, nice little six pack, a nice ride, or something when he get out and flex a little you know. Because women like to talk, they generally tell you everything you need to know to determine whether she is dating or booty call material. I ask a woman the question "What can you do for me that I can't do for myself." This basically let's me determine her standards like if she's religious etc. The wrong answer to this questions would be something like she's a good cook, cleans good, awesome sex etc. These types of responses don't mean anything to me. A man can tell in the first 30 minutes whether the woman is relationship material by the responses she gives to questions he asks like: What's your story? He's basically looking for her to tell him about herself. He's looking to see if she has any problems.

1. Why you not with nobody right now? The right responses would be something like the guy was a knucklehead. The wrong responses would be talking about her past relationships and the types of dudes she's had to break up with.
2. What do you do?
3. How many kids do you have?
4. Do you go to Church?

He's also looking to see if she's high maintenance.

Bachelor #4 response: Both. It depends on what you're looking for that night. If you go to a club and you're a little tipsy, it's lust. But if you're out somewhere and you inadvertently bump into someone, they spark your curiosity, and upon a further preponderance of the information that is given to you, at that moment it may be love. Cause like I said, love is a feeling and you can feel like you love someone and it can be a false feeling. I don't think you should have do's and don'ts. I don't like limits. I don't like time frames. I don't like rules. Do what feels right to you, what's happy to you, as long as no one is going to get hurt. So I guess that would be the rule. Do whatever your heart feel as so long it's not going to hurt yourself or someone else and that's for both men and women.

Bachelor #5 response: Generally it's lust. Because you don't know anything about the person to love em. So what you're basing any thoughts of moving forward on? Of course, in some settings it could be on

Chapter Two – *Rules of Dating*

something they said or done. It's not that you're walking into it saying ooh this is my wife! Oooh I just can't wait to have babies with her. No, you're thinking about doing the process that it takes to make babies, but you're not talking about marrying her because you found her that attractive. Anybody that talk about" it was love at first site," is really just blowing smoke up your ass. Cause really, it was lust that eventually turned into love, but it really was just that.

Question 25: What is business card pimpin/playing?

Bachelor #1 response: I can relate to business card player. That's someone whose putting it out there.

Bachelor #4 response: I'm not exactly sure, but what I believe that is when you conjure up a business card depicting yourself to be something that maybe you're not necessarily. I think it's big in Atlanta with the music industry or the modeling agency. A person may give you a business card that they're such a such and from such and such agency, and they can help you do this, and that, when in reality they just want the opportunity to impress you, to get you to believe they're something that their not, and definitely to have the opportunity to see you again. Actually Ms. Right now just went through that with a couple of people in Atlanta because she is a model. A gentleman approached her with a card telling her all this wonderful stuff about how he could help her and get her in some videos. And she recently sent me a correspondence that he sent her via instant messenger basically saying that he hopes that they can pursue something on a more personal level and he'll know how to keep business and pleasure separate and that sort of thing. Where I would think that would be business card pimping to catch or to grab the attention of the opposite sex.

Question 26: To judge or be judged (what are some things that make you uninterested in her no matter what)

Bachelor #1 response: If there are too many kids involved, I'm definitely, not interested. I don't' care what she working with, what she got, what she's accomplished, I'm not interested. I honestly feel with a lot of baby daddy's, there's a lot of drama involved. Cause the average man if he's not in the kid's life at that particular time. As soon as a real man steps up to the plate, he wants to play daddy all of a sudden. Then you gone have issues and I don't want to deal with those kinds of issues. Am I missing out on something great, possibly? Am I willing to take that chance, no. Anybody that wants kids, I'm not interested. I'm at a point in my life now I don't want any kids. If they have some that's fine, wanting another one, that's definitely out of the question.

Chapter Two – *Rules of Dating*

Bachelor #4 response: A man can have too many baby mommas if he frivolously has sex with women and has babies with them and has no intent to be with them, But if a man or woman honestly got themselves in that situation where a baby was produced with the intent of being with that person and it just didn't work out, I don't think you can have too many baby mommas/daddies because as long as you're willing to give yourself to someone in that fashion, where you're going raw, unprotected, and you're willing to consummate the relationship, and you have that type of trust in that person, then I don't think it's a bad thing. I can't see it being a negative. Whereas someone that has three or four baby mommas or daddies because they like to have sex, and they're not responsible to put on a condom, and they don't know the person, then that type of person may. I judge people solely on their reasoning because I think everything has a reason. Like I said, the rules of dating is to do whatever your heart's content. If you're doing something because you believe it's going to make you happy, I have no problem with it. But if your rationale is your doing things because it's to the exception of everyone else like when a woman tells me she can't have sex with me tonight because it's too soon and I say to you okay do you want to have sex with me and they say yes, then I'm gonna judge you because you live your life for the approval of everybody else, and that's someone that I don't want to deal with. Now if you say I don't want to have sex with you tonight and that's why I'm not, I can respect that. So I judge a person based on their rationale, their reasoning for doing things and their ability or inability to tell the truth.

Question 27: Quit Faking

Bachelor #1 response: The average person, if you wait until 6 or 7:00. in the afternoon to go out on a date, you know you haven't ate anything cause you basically waiting on the dinner date then you get there and all you order is a salad or a grilled chicken or something! You know you hungry. You know then later on that evening we gotta go to the movies and I got to listen to your stomach growl all night long. I'm like nah, eat. I always ask to look at pictures. You know whether it's a photo album, a picture in your wallet, so I basically want to see the real you. The average person you go out with, they done did theyself up basically. I have a habit if I'm going out at 7:00 I'm showing up at 6:00 so I can basically see you before you get yourself together. I really don't like the weave; I don't care for the fake nails. I don't care for too much make up. I honestly feel that a woman should take pride in her appearance, but to me, all that stuff, you becoming somebody that you not, and if you can't maintain that then you faking the funk.

Chapter Two – *Rules of Dating*

Bachelor #4 response: If you're out with a person and you take them back to a house, hotel or whatever; and it's clear to you and that person what both of you want, and that person acts as if that's not what they want just because they don't want you to think that they're easy because it's so soon. I think that's faking. To portray an image of yourself that is not accurate, that's faking. A lot of people go to the club and they go to the bar, and they pull out a whop full of money with a couple of hundred dollar bills on top but underneath it aint' nothing but singles; that's faking. They want you to think they're rich but they really just spent their whole paycheck. You go to the club every weekend, and you buy a new outfit every weekend it appears to people that you're enjoying yourself but you're really out there looking for a man. You done spent every bit of money you got hoping somebody's going to rescue you; you faking. A woman that goes to the restaurant with you and nitpicks over her food because she don't want you to think she's a slob; that's faking. If you're hungry you better eat it. Hair, nails, me personally, I don't like makeup but I don't necessarily think that's faking because if that's who you are, then that's cool. You're not necessarily somebody that I will be attracted to but if that's who you are, that's cool. A lot of different people do a lot of different things to beautify themselves; hair and nails being one. I have no problem with that. I don't necessarily think it's faking just as long as you don't portray them to be your own, and you don't say hey these are my nails and I can say the acrylic and you don't say hey this is my hair and I can see the weave glue. That type of thing is when it becomes faking when you portray it to be something that it's not.

Question 28: Seeing right through the madness

Bachelor #1 response: Seeing right through the madness, is basically someone like I said again, you know the average female think she got it all together, and some do, but some feel that they got what it takes to pull you in that relationship mode, and they'll pull all the tricks out the bag; you know they try to do this, they'll do all that, they freak you a little bit, you know, they figure all that's gone move you, and you might every now and then, you might slip up and say that "L" word on em. Me I don't do that personally, but it might slip out on the average brother. And once you say that L word, they feel they got you, but basically they done got theyself.

Bachelor #4 response: I weigh what a person says against what they do. A lot of people will try to sell you a dream. The madness would be the dream. What I basically do being the analytical person that I am, I break everything you say, and or do, down to the smallest type of understanding so that whenever something comes up that contradicts something that you've previously said and or did, then a question is raised. Now if that is

Chapter Two – *Rules of Dating*

true, then why did you say this or if that is true, why did you do this. Now based on your answer, I'm gonna know based on my own intuition, I'm gonna believe that whether you're trying to sell me a dream or create madness or if you're really being truthful.

Question 29: What are some turn on's, turn off's

Bachelor #4 response: Confidence is sexy. Neatness is very sexy. Skin is sexy. Butts are sexy, breasts are sexy, turn ons rather. Lips are turn ons. How they walk, I think anyone with a very positive ambiance about themselves is very sexy. Intelligence is my ultimate. A person that fakes it is a turn off. Fat that is not inherent like a person that is naturally big boned is not fat to me. A person that don't care about themselves or their personal health is a turn off. A person that don't care about their appearance is a turn off.

Question 30: How can a woman tell when he's not interested? No call, no show.

_____

_____

_____

Question 31: Name some mood setting techniques

Bachelor #1 response: When a female comes to my house and she walks through the door and she hears some Luther, some Teddy P playing in the background. I got some wine cheese and crackers sitting on the table. I got some massage oil sitting there, its dark, and some scented candles. It's got to be scented candles. I done took a little bath, put on a light coat of baby oil on myself, and got my chest glistening a little bit. Got on my silk PJ's walking round chillin; you know, that's basically setting the mood. Though when she walk through the door, she know it's on for the night. Not necessarily a street booty call or nothing like that, but some love making finna happen that night.

Chapter Two – *Rules of Dating*

Question 32: What are the different levels of intimacy and define them

Bachelor #1 response: There are three levels to the booty:
1. Sex: She gets just a little bit but not consistently. Sometimes I may kiss her but not regularly
2. Fuck: Not pleasurable. 3 pumps and I'm done.
3. Love Making: When he's truly trying to please her

Question 33: Too much, too fast, too soon

Bachelor #1 response: That's definitely a no no. A lot of women have a tendency to give up too much and what that does, that takes you out of relationship mode. You have to realize that a man might be trying to push up on you physically and you might want to real bad, but as soon as you give in without setting ground rules, your giving up too much too soon, too fast and basically what ends up happening is, you become street booty. And that's just the bottom line. Same thing with a man, he can have a tendency to spend, spend, spend, spend, spend, spend, spend all his money and never learn to use the word no, and that would cause problems in the long run if it ever goes to become a relationship because once you tell her yes, she's gone always want that answer.

Question 34: What is your definition of a booty call?

Bachelor #1 response: A booty call is basically a situation when the female knows exactly what's going on. It's already predetermined what's happening. Its mutual friends that have been intimate once upon a time so they basically know what time it is. It's normally late; 10 or 11:00 at night. No strings attached. Just get in and get out. No cuddling, or holding, and none of that stuff is happening. Just basically getting your oil lubed.

Question 35: Explain dates on rotation

Bachelor #1 response: Been there, done that. Rotating dates is when you basically have it like an assembly line. Me personally, I try to track my women's cycles. I find out whose period falls when, and how, and that's how they get dates basically. The average brother won't go to that extent. Me myself, I try to keep everything moving right along so there's no blockage, no back up you know. The assembly line keeps moving.

Chapter Two – *Rules of Dating*

Question 36: Is it good for men/women to pitch a tent until their ready to buy a house when it comes to sex?

Bachelor #1 response: Pitching a tent for a man is an excellent thing due to the fact that he's getting the best of both worlds. For a female, it's basically dogging her out a little bit because the average brother is not going to ever marry her if he finds out that she's pitching a tent. She basically have to leave the city wherever she was doing all this stuff in and go someplace else to establish a home. Pitching a tent right here in Rochester is too small. To many T-Pee's up you know what I'm saying. You pitch a tent over here, you got a T-Pee right next to you.

Question 37: Is it okay for a woman to call a man for a booty call?

_____

_____

_____

Question 38: Why do you think women are settling to be booty call dates?

_____

_____

_____

Question 39: Sweet equity or Hope Exploiters what is it?

Bachelor #1 response: When a man dates a woman for more than three (3) months and strings her along letting her believe that their relationship is a lot more than just dating; then he's exploiting her. He should be man enough to let her know that he stills like her as a friend and that he's not interested in anything more than that.

Chapter Two – *Rules of Dating*

Question 40: How important is a woman's sexual past to a man?

_____

_____

_____

Question 41: How many sexual partners is acceptable for a woman to have?

_____

_____

_____

DELBRA BARR
CHAPTER TWO: RULES OF DATING REFLECTION
THAT WAS THEN (2004)

In chapter two, the bachelors were able to help me identify things they looked for in order to determine whether you could be someone he'd like to get to know better, or whether or not you're just good to "hit it and quit it." If a woman isn't true to what she really wants, and doesn't let it be known, then she's going to find herself compromising what she wants in an attempt to lure him into giving her what she needs. All of the bachelors realized that women are emotional beings. Some used it to get what they wanted. Some embraced it until they determined that the woman was going to use it against them. All in all, I've come to respect men more because I understand now that they really know and understand women better than we know ourselves. The women's movement got us to change our way of thinking about everything, but it didn't change men's views about dating and relationships. Some men in 2005 still wanted to hold on to that old traditional way of thinking where a man has the "good" woman at home who took care of him and the family; and yet when he really wanted to get his freak on, he knew he wouldn't be getting it on at home. Unfortunately, in 2004, they're dating "new millennium women" who enjoy their sensuality and sexuality. Women who are now being punished if they have even a little hint of "freak" in her. Men are enjoying the freedom to be sensual and sexual with women because they are in touch with their sexuality; however, the only thing she's getting is sex because he doesn't take her serious if she appears to have too many sexual encounters.

On the other hand, there are women who want to "think like a man," but they've forgotten how to "treat a man like a man." As one of the bachelors pointed out, "how can a woman know how to play the game if she can't even equate the numbers the same"? Men sexual encounters outnumber women almost 2-3 times to her 1, so how can she play a game she can't even compete in. Women need to stop trying to show the man she can be the "man" in her household. A man wants to feel as if he's contributing to her life and their lifestyle. He was to know that she has faith in him, and she believes he will do what it takes to protect and nurture his family. If he can't do that, then he won't stay around. I've dating some beautiful men and even if they weren't the man for me, I appreciated the person that they were. Some were still trying to find themselves. I remember someone once told me when I asked him why he couldn't find himself by establishing a relationship with me. He said "I look up to you! I need someone who looks up to me." Even though I understood the statement, I definitely didn't agree with it, but if that's what he felt he needed, then he was entitled to that. Women have to stop trying to help a man find himself. Only until he does it for himself, can he ever appreciate the woman in his life and by his side.

MRS DEBBIE CAKES
CHAPTER TWO: RULES OF DATING REFLECTION
THIS IS NOW (2017)

In order for women to truly know how to determine if the man she is dating is a great partner for her, she has to learn how to love herself first. Unfortunately women have never been told HOW to love themselves. Women have been encouraged to believe that her self-esteem and her purpose in life is to give to others selfishly and she will find love through the process. So women give, and give, and give, and in the end, they find themselves feeling alone, and empty. She feels like no one understands them, and others take them for granted. The first step in loving a man is to know how to love yourself. Your sense of worth can't be found through other's expectation of you. Read the book If I Can't Be The Cake, I Won't Be The Crumz in order to define your 80/20. 80 is the minimum you need to be happy, and 20 is the maximum you will compromise. When you find yourself compromising more than 20%, then you feel unhappy, unloved and frustrated or a crumzy situation.

Now, after you have determined what you need to be happy, then you can read the behavior of others to see if you can support their views and expectations. If you can, then everything will be peaches and cream. If you can't, then you can respect them for who they are while setting strong, healthy boundaries to keep them from making you feel unhappy or crumzy. Once I learned how to do that, I learned how to walk away from a relationship that was toxic for me. I could be friends or friendly with someone even if our views were not alike. Dating is not an application for a mini marriage. It is a way to determine how you can relate to others. It is a way to communicate and socialize with someone but in order for you to do that successfully, you have to give the process some time. Don't be in a hurry to get a title before you have determined if they are worthy of your heart and that process takes time.

CHAPTER TWO: RULES OF DATING - MY FAVORITE QUOTES

But if it's going well and if I honestly feel that she's worth another date, I might let her call me in a couple days. But would I call her, definitely not. p. 53

But you shouldn't be relying on her to provide you transportation for the date. p. 54

Women, don't waste our money. p. 54

Because women like to talk, they generally tell you everything you need to know to determine whether she is dating or booty call material. p. 55

The wrong answer to this questions would be something like she's a good cook, cleans good, awesome sex etc. p. 55

I basically want to see the real you. p. 57

They want you to think they're rich but they really just spent their whole paycheck. p. 58

You done spent every bit of money you got hoping somebody's going to rescue you; you faking. p. 58

And once you say that L word, they feel they got you, but basically they done got theyself.p. 58

A lot of women have a tendency to give up too much and what that does, that takes you out of relationship mode. p. 60

As soon as you give in without setting ground rules, your giving up too much too soon, too fast and basically what ends up happening is, you become street booty. p. 61

The average brother is not going to ever marry her if he finds out that she's pitching a tent. p. 61

He should be man enough to let her know that he stills like her as a friend and that he's not interested in anything more than that. p. 61

Chapter Two – *Rules of Dating*

KEEP DOING

START DOING

STOP DOING

Chapter 3
Tips about establishing/maintaining a relationship

Chapter 3
Tips about establishing/maintaining a relationship

The purpose for the questions identified in this section was to get the bachelors to help women understand what they felt were important techniques for establishing a long, lasting relationship with a man. I regret I did not get the chance to ask them many of the questions I knew as a woman would be important to know like "why do men cheat," and what would a woman need to do in order to help her man feel secure in his relationship with her. Because the new millennium woman was not going to listen to her mother or her grandmother about how to maintain a relationships because we had seen many of the women in or lives and even those portrayed on television as women who were mentally, psychologically, emotionally, financially, and even physically abused so how could the women in our lives provide us relationship advice when it appeared they need some themselves.

Many older women grew up during a time when men were supposed to be the provider and her role was to take care of the home, the children, and the family so she never learned how to take care of herself because everyone else needed her to take care of them first. Many of these women maintained long lasting relationships but at a great personal and self-sacrificial price because once her children had grown up and left home, when they became empty nesters, she had never learned how to have a connection or a relationship with her husband so she found herself feeling alone and isolated, and he never put time, energy, and effort into building the relationship with his wife, so it was easy for him to leave her and the family in search of his proclaimed need for happiness. The new millennium woman learned how to see their relationship as dysfunctional so she knew she did not want to be unhappy for the sake of everyone else. However, she never learned how to understand him as a man so when she threw out traditional roles in the relationship to take on a new modern approach, she didn't realize the damage it would cause to the man's identity and his ego and the hit to relating with men because the rules of the game had changed, but no one had the new instruction manual.

Chapter 3 - *Tips about establishing/maintaining a relationship*

Question 42: Define Relationship

Bachelor #1 response: Relationship is two individuals. If you look at the last part of relationships you have a ship. A ship is nothing but a vessel. A relationship is basically a ship; that if you find the vessel you like, you gotta make sure this vessel is able to carry you where you need to be. Withstand a storm if it get a little rocky at times, and sometimes that vessel doesn't have to look good on the outside but be sound on the inside.

Question 43: What is the man/woman's role in relationships?

_____

_____

_____

Question 44: What types/levels of Relationships are there?

Bachelor #1 response: When there is no established "relationship," then there are no obligations from each party to be committed to the other. They can't get mad if there's no calls, or you don't go by. She shouldn't be assuming we're "together." The brother has to come right out and let her know what time it is. If she asks him whether they are committed and he seems evasive, then he's not ready for a relationship. She should just jump ship because she's sailing on a boat that has no life preserve! A ship is a vessel; I'm looking to see if that ship can take me where I need to go. If you can't handle the ride, then don't get on it. I'm looking to see if it can withstand the storm or will it break up if it gets a little rocky! There are strictly sex relationships, there's the platonic friend, booty call, intimate relationships, and then there are the just trying to get to know you relationships where somebody could possibly be relationship material where you're trying to spend a little extra quality time with an individual.

1. Friends: no sex. Just general conversation about life and each other's relationship. They each do what they want to do and vice versa. The rules seem to always change. There's no changing the rules.
2. Chillin and kickin it: Open dialogue about sex and everything else.
3. Real Good Friends: Sex at least once but still able to chill and kickin.
4. Bed Buddies: Getting together for movies, dinner and frequent encounters of sex but no series commitment
5. Relationship. If you're feeling someone, don't be afraid to let them know. Set the ground rules going in and stick to them

Chapter 3 - *Tips about establishing/maintaining a relationship*

Question 45: What must be established in order for a man to acknowledge he's in a relationship?

> **Bachelor #1 response**: The ground rules need to be established in any friendship, platonic relationship, whatever because what happens, when the ground rules are established they know exactly what to expect.

Question 46: What are the ingredients for a great relationship?

_____

_____

_____

Question 47: What are the ingredients for a disastrous relationship?

_____

_____

_____

Question 48: Ready for sex, but what about commitment

> **Bachelor #1 response**: Man is always ready for sex. Commitment that's on the back burner. Female is the opposite she figures once sex is given, commitment should be established at particular time when it's over. A man does not think that way, basically the commitment is out the door once a woman gives herself to a man. The ground rules need to be established. In any friendship, platonic relationship or whatever the grounds are established. When the ground rules are established they know exactly what's happening, but if they have to assume what the rules are, that's why it's so easy for a man to get in and get out because commitment is never established. That way he can say they we was just friends when a female starts to trip. Like being just friends is a situation when a man can just do what he wanta do without you trippin if you see him with somebody else. Men mix friendship with commitment because they allow the female to take it there without them actually saying it. A female will take it to a relationship level without actually talking about it so a man can just assume I can play this relationship game but it was never talked about so

Chapter 3 - *Tips about establishing/maintaining a relationship*

when she trip out I can through that right back at her we just friends, when did this become a relationship you never told me nothing. In other words, the rules got changed, but the rule book was never handed out to the brother.

Question 49: Do men what a sexually experienced woman as his wife?

_____

_____

_____

Question 50: Why do men cheat?

_____

_____

_____

Question 51: Can and should your relationship survive if he/she cheated?

_____

_____

_____

Question 52: Will a man say he loves her and lie?

Bachelor #1 response: Oh yeah. Would I, no. The average brother, yeah. That "L" word will take you places. Just like the L-train. That "L" word will take you to a relationship level without you actually having to say relationship. It'll get the freak out of some women; it'll get money out of some women, car keys out of some women, house keys out of some women. Cause the average woman don't even know what love is.

Chapter 3 - *Tips about establishing/maintaining a relationship*

Question 53: When he says he's not ready, does he really mean it?

Bachelor #1 response: Yep. Does a woman take it that way, nope. The average woman feel he's just a little nervous, a little scared a little shy of commitment but if it works out he's going to come around. But if a brother says he's not ready for commitment, take that to heart because that's what he means. The average man is going to mean what he says and says what he means. The average woman is not hearing that and that's too bad. She'll hear a lie before she hear the truth and that's too bad.

Question 54: What needs to be in place in order for a man/woman to feel they're in love/committed relationship/ready for marriage?

_____

_____

_____

Question 55: Do you believe in soul mates?

_____

_____

_____

Question 56: Do men really "listen" to women when they are talking?

_____

_____

_____

Chapter 3 - *Tips about establishing/maintaining a relationship*

Question 57: Do mean really hear women when they say they're upset?

_____

_____

_____

Question 58: Does good sex justify B.S. or a relationship?

Bachelor #1 response: It all depends on the individual. Some women will put up with a lot of foolishness because they're getting their tune up right, and the same thing for the average brother. A man can get pussy whipped to where he just loose his mind. He'll take anything he can from a woman. He'll take a whole bunch of B.S. because the sex is great. But what he fails to realize, the same way she's freaking him, she got to be freaking the next man. If the brother is putting it down like that, there's got to be a lot more where that comes from. Why do you think there's so many young brothers taking Viagra now. Yes sir. The average brother wants to feel he's Mandingo. That they can put it down like that, hour after hour, after hour. You got to understand the younger generation of men feels that a woman wants to be pounded two to three hours. I honestly feel that a good hour is all you need.

Question 59: What are some things a man can do to get a woman in the mood when she's not?

Bachelor #1 response: First of all, a man can't feel like he's eager to have sex. A man got to figure I'm taking the time to stimulate this woman's mind, body, as well as her soul. You know possibly with a back rub and me personally, I will allow a woman to get butt naked; but will never ever once try to get physical with her. Cause I honestly feel that it has to be her decision. I don't want to feel like I'm trying to coax her into doing something or trying to bribe her into doing something or making her feel like ok we're naked now we might as well do something. I've turned down the booty at times that way it'll make them want me instead of me wanting them. Cause first of all, if you stimulate a woman's mind, the body is basically yours. She'll find herself saying "you know this Negro took the time to give me a backrub and never once asked for none. He know I'm laying here and after we got done he said you go on and cover up or whatever. I'm going downstairs to get us some wine or something. By the time you come back up, she hot and bothered and ready to get this thang, you know set her off. So basically, you have to

Chapter 3 - *Tips about establishing/maintaining a relationship*

stimulate her mind first. You can't make her think that it's strictly physical. You got to make her think that you care truly about her feelings, and what she truly wants, and not what she's being made to do or be coaxed into it. Can you dig it?

DELBRA BARR
CHAPTER THREE: REFLECTION - TIPS ABOUT ESTABLISHING/MAINTAINING A RELATIONSHIP THAT WAS THEN (2004)

Women often try to rationalize why men do what they do. In my research for this book, I stumbled across a book that said it so well. If he didn't call, it's because he didn't want to. If he didn't come over, it's because he didn't want to. If he forgot your birthday, it's because he didn't care to remember. Just as I discovered the bachelors knew women almost better than they knew themselves, they know what we need emotionally to feel connected to them. They may not want us to feel connected so instead of being a man about it, they like knowing they have women on rotation and if we take that away from them, then we take away the fun. They do things knowing we will react to them. Just enough to keep us at bay, in pocket, clinging on, but not enough to cause us to storm out the door. The best thing a woman can do is to establish some boundaries, limitations and stick to them. Men like seeing whether they can get away with the dumbest thing.

On my first date with a guy, he took me to an adult video store. Internally, I was having a fit because I could tell he was just trying to see if I'd go along with it. You know, to see if my no's would mean yes. I should've stopped talking to him after that but noooooo. We are associates today, when I thought about our intention, when I first met him, I sized him up, he looked nice, dressed good, sounded very educated and professional so I thought he exemplified the type of guy I would like to date; you know to see if we could lay the grounds for a long lasting relationship. However, if I would've gone in that store, I would've set an impression of me that I was willing to be looked upon as a "conquest" and not a woman of standards.

I could tell he was trying to set me up, but I was truly naïve to not feel disrespected because his actions were clearly for Ms. Right Now, but I didn't know how to see it as that. I thought it was just a "test" and not a sign for my position with him of just a conquest. Men like to see just how far they can push us. How far we will let them go. Only until I met with the bachelors was I able to see their truth for what it is and not what I wanted it to be. It's taken me a long time to figure that one out!

MRS DEBBIE CAKES
CHAPTER THREE: REFLECTION - TIPS ABOUT
ESTABLISHING/MAINTAINING A RELATIONSHIP
THIS IS NOW (2017)

How do we learn how to love ourselves, while at the same time, love others? That became the new "norm" for establishing a healthy, long lasting relationship. Each individual has to start with themselves before they can ever build a relationship with someone. You can't find happiness through the happiness of others because you will find yourself on an emotional rollercoaster. If they're happy, you're happy. If they're sad, you're sad. Never put others above yourself, and most importantly, never put others above your faith. Women need to learn how to be like men when it comes to giving herself to someone. If he don't stick around to find out whether or not the wait is worth it, then nothing lost, nothing gained.

People scoffed at the concept of the book *Men are from Mars, and Women are from Venus*, but for me, the book did exactly what the author wanted it to do. It educated me about how men think and respond to people and their issues, and it taught me how to support men, while at the same time understand if I respond differently than he does, that I'm not to tear him down because of it. I learned how to support him when he needed to go to his "cave" and how to support him when I could tell he was having an emotional crisis. Even though it might be a woman's human nature to support and cheer them on, we have to respect the notion that he just needs time to process what's going on and when he's ready he'll share it with us.

I also learned the importance of setting boundaries with men, and that they want to see more women exemplifying and even demanding higher standards for themselves and from the people who are in their lives. When women raise the bar, then we will collectively cause them to do the same. But when women lower the bar and their expectations from men, all they are doing is giving them exactly what they want in the first place, which is to play with as many women as they can until they are ready to settle down and unfortunately when they get ready to settle down, he will be looking for a woman in the future and not from a conquest he had in his past.

Ladies, take the time to think about the guys you have "dated" and have been intimate with. When you think about their actions, the words they've said, or the fact that in the end, regardless of your intention, the relationship ends anyway. When we have the tools to discern a person's intentions, we empower ourselves with the knowledge of how to stop feeling like a piece of meat in a sea of piranhas. No More Crumz in 2018 and beyond. Read the book, *"If I Can't Be The Cake, I Won't Be the Crumz"* in any edition to learn how to establish healthy boundaries with people who are different than you. You can't change someone, you can only influence them. And you definitely can't raise a grown boy into a man. However; if enough women start demanding more, they will have no choice but to give more.

CHAPTER THREE: REFLECTION - TIPS ABOUT ESTABLISHING/MAINTAINING A RELATIONSHIP
MY FAVORITE QUOTES

A relationship is basically a ship; that if you find the vessel you like, you gotta make sure this vessel is able to carry you where you need to be. p. 69

If she asks him whether they are committed and he seems evasive, then he's not ready for a relationship. p. 69

Man is always ready for sex. Commitment that's on the back burner. p. 70

When she trip out I can through that right back at her we just friends, when did this become a relationship you never told me nothing. The rules got changed, but the rule book was never handed out to the brother. p. 71

That "L" word will take you places. It'll get the freak out of some women; it'll get money out of some women, car keys out of some women, house keys out of some women. p. 71

But if a brother says he's not ready for commitment, take that to heart because that's what he means. p. 72

She'll hear a lie before she hear the truth and that's too bad. p. 72

Question 3 - *Tips about establishing/maintaining a relationship*

KEEP DOING

_____

_____

_____

_____

_____

_____

START DOING

_____

_____

_____

_____

_____

STOP DOING

_____

_____

_____

_____

_____

Chapter 4
After the Love is Gone

Chapter 4
After the Love is Gone

What do you do when the person you have give your time, energy, emotional space, and body too no longer wants to be with you? Heartache, after heartache, after heartache, women have to learn how to change their unhealthy dating practices if they want to be in a long, lasting relationship but when you settle for crumz, you will nine times out of 10 find yourself in a crumzy situation. Now there have been some women who have turned their crumzy situation into a crumb cake. I'm not saying it is impossible, but for those women who have not been successful at settling for less to get more, when you realize you have once again been intimate with someone that you have to now remove the emotional ties you thought you had with that person is painful to do.

When a man says he's done, he really means he's done. It is possible for him to want to get together, but during the process when you are being rejected, and they cut off all forms of communication from you because they no longer desire to talk to you, see, text, or message you. You feel a sense of helplessness, loneliness, and rejection. The reason they are gone is because there were so many signs that you ignored that the end was inevitable. I regret I never asked the bachelors the questions outlined in this section, but feel free to ask the men in your life. Let their answers help to confirm your need to think differently about who you chose to give yourself intimately too.

Chapter 4 - *After the Love is Gone*

Question 60: What are some things what women do to mess up the relationship?

_____

Question 61: Is having someone better than no one at all?

Bachelor #1 response: Nope. Cause you can have someone but what does that mean if that person is empty, cold, blank, confused, and they could be dramatized. I would rather be by myself than with somebody I got to figure out every day. See the average female doesn't feel that way. The average female got to have somebody. But when its winter time, the average brother is going to settle in and that's a true fact. The average brother that was single all summer will have him a girlfriend, and be in a relationship, living in somebody's house, driving somebody's car, and he'll be there until the first week of April. He'll last through Valentine's Day, he'll last through Christmas, New Years, but come April, he'll pick a fight and get kicked out.

Question 62: Abusive relationships, what makes men abuse their mate?

_____

Question 63: Knowing when the honeymoon's over. Why do people stay in relationships where they love someone who doesn't love them back?

_____

Question 64: Name some break up techniques

_____

Question 65: Friends no more. How do men really deal with break ups?

_____

DELBRA BARR
CHAPTER FOUR: REFLECTION – AFTER THE LOVE IS GONE
THAT WAS THEN (2004)

When a woman has been intimate with a man, one of the hardest thing for her to face is when she has to break up and with him and find a way to move on with a clear conscious. When this happened to me, I was always able to walk away with my head held high because I knew I went into the situation for the right reason. I understood that I had a very unhealthy understanding about men, dating, and what I expectations should've been when trying to establish a relationship with someone, and even though it had to end, I was always a lady, I took care of my daughter, I sheltered as best I could when I saw things weren't going as I planned, and I walked away maintaining a healthy friendship or association with them. Back then, I didn't know I was getting played. But in 2004, I realize I needed to change my views about men, and how I communicated with others. The change had to start with me and now that I had a different perspective, I was going to do what needed to be done for me to fix ALL of the unhealthy relationships in my life.

My communication issues were not only with men, they were with family members, relatives, coworkers, my ex-husband, and practically everyone in my life. I needed to understand what I was doing wrong so that I could fix me. Once I could start with me, and then the issues that existed with my family/relatives, I could stop the world from hurting me. Through this process, I realized my hurts actually stemmed from my childhood and the unhealthy communication and relationships that existed in my family. If I could stop my family from hurting me, then I could definitely stop those who were not related to me through DNA. The issue is not necessarily that the love ended. It is because you haven't figured out how to identify what is really the problem and each party work collectively to fix it. What I found to be at the heart of the problem was my holding in and suppressing my "truth."

If someone was hurting me emotionally or psychologically, I wouldn't tell them because I didn't want them to get upset, or I knew they would and so I would avoid it. Many times I could tell when someone was doing something on purpose, just to have their way, but I didn't think I had a voice so I just let it slide. You know, let it roll off my back. Each time I suppressed a concern, that concern just joined the many others I had been suppressing until I couldn't take it anymore. The love isn't gone. Communicating the hurts you feel sabotage the loving feeling. When we communicate effectively, the love can heal all of our wounds. But if we don't know how to speak about our issues, then the pain over rides the love we have. It's still there, just not at the top or the focus of our emotions.

MRS DEBBIE CAKES
CHAPTER FOUR: REFLECTION – AFTER THE LOVE IS GONE
THIS IS NOW (2017)

The reason relationships fail is because we haven't learned how to get passed that period in the relationship when the real work begin. My grandmother had a saying *"1st Month Sugar, 2nd Month Pie, 3rd Month Go To Hell, Damn You and Die."* Over time, I began to realize that 2nd month phase is that period in the relationship when we have to learn how to deal with;

1) transitioning through life's issues,
2) determining if we have what it takes to communicate through a rough patch,
3) patience and long suffering.

When you have been offended and hurt by a person and you have never learned how to communicate those feelings to that person, you allow your hurts to build up to the point where you eventually explode, and once you have exploded you don't care how you hurt them because you don't feel they care that they have hurt you. Many times the person doesn't understand why you have been offended and their inability to sympathize with you or to understand your feelings cause you to feel even more offended and hurt. Women have to understand that men do not "intentionally" hurt you; they just don't know how to help resolve the problem when you are emotional. Women have to learn how to define what they need and then how to articulate that to their partner. If they don't articulate or communicate well, they will find themselves either single, alone, or abusers. Just because you are hurting, that does not give you the right to verbally abuse others. If a man finds it difficult to communicate with you, they will leave you. And when they leave, women don't realize they have contributed to the problem. It is easy to point the finger at others, than to realize you have been a contributor to the issue. The issue is not that the love is gone; it is they have not learned how to communicate through the rough patch. When a woman learns how to communicate with them in a way the man can respond, she will find herself obtaining the results she'd been praying for from me. Many times women find themselves single because they haven't learned this valuable lesson.

MY FAVORITE QUOTE

I would rather be by myself than with somebody I got to figure out every day. p. 81

He'll last through Valentine's Day, he'll last through Christmas, New Years, but come April, he'll pick a fight and get kicked out. p. 81

Chapter 4 - *After the Love is Gone*

KEEP DOING

_____

_____

_____

_____

_____

_____

START DOING

_____

_____

_____

_____

_____

_____

STOP DOING

_____

_____

_____

_____

_____

Chapter 5
Religion & Dating, is it possible?

Chapter 5
Religion & Dating, is it possible?

From 1984 until I got married on January 31, 2009 I have always been a Christian woman dating and it was definitely a painful journey because the Church does not know how to effectively handle dating and religion. Single people just like the church understand what the Bible says about fornication and all of the other scriptures that speak to the plight that single faith based believers experience everyday but instead of judgment, they need tools, guidance, support, and direction during this transitional period in their life. When I was single and going to the church Elim Christian Fellowship on Main Street, God put in my heart to start a singles ministry and through the support of our lay pastor, Pastor Tracy, I set out to prayerfully figure out what the Bible says about dating. I bought study Bibles, searched online, and I even fasted hoping that God would help me understand how singles Christian should date which would lead them to marriage. There word "date" or "dating" is not in the Bible. People were single, married, or widowed. There are no other forms of relationships listed so after fasting, praying, and meditating on what a single Christian should be doing based on the readings in I Corinthians 7, I realized when you are single, that is the season in your life when you can devote a great deal of your time to working on yourself, your family, and in the ministry. I appreciated the support that the lay pastor gave me, but I came to realize if the shepherd of the house does not support the vision for the singles ministry, no one else in the church would so even though I passed out flyers and personally went to people individually sharing with them about the ministry, because it was never announced during service, and because the deacons and other pastors never announced support for the ministry, no one attended. Just because the "church" does not know or have a process for helping people deal with crumzy situations in their life that are against the Word of God, that does not mean He won't provide the church with someone who is willing to take up the charge and through Him, provide a process of healing for those going through the storms of life.

The church has a strong ministerial plan for the children, the women, the men, and the married couples but when 70% of the congregation is single women with children, that is a large population of people forced to take on humanistic views about their singleness because the church has checked out from the process of providing them the direction they need. The questions outlined in this section are a great start for singles to begin asking the leaders, elders, ministers, and pastors in their church so they can create a spiritual home where they can be fed in the areas of their life where it is needed the most.

Chapter 5 – *Religion & Dating, is it possible?*

Question 66: Single and trying to be Christ like, why is that so hard?

_____

_____

Question 67: Looking for a soul mate in the church. Is that so wrong?

_____

_____

Question 68: On the prowl in church. Men/women looking for single church going mates

_____

_____

Question 69: What does it mean to be equally yoked and can two people really be it?

_____

_____

Question 70: Ministering to singles: Why is it missing?

_____

_____

DELBRA BARR
CHAPTER FIVE: RELIGION AND DATING, IS IT POSSIBLE?
REFLECTION

THAT WAS THEN (2004)

After my meeting with the bachelors, I received the great revelation that men loved and appreciated women who went to church and many times, preyed upon those women because they at least desired to have a foundation in their life that was based on spiritual values, morals and ethics. However, women of God have to learn how to not allow their faith to be used as a woman against them. God set boundaries with us and he does not give us all of the desires of our heart because either we aren't ready to handle what we are asking for, or it is not His will for us. Stop believing just because you prayed for it, it will happen. If it's His will, than it will happen. If It's not, it won't. Learn how to love yourself even though you are single. Your singleness is not a curse, but is only a season. I realized He didn't allow the relationships I had in the past because after my daughter was born, I prayed earnestly asking him to not let me get pregnant by someone who would not be my husband, or the person He wanted for me and that prayer was answered. There were many times I was afraid I was pregnant by someone I knew the situation was not a desirable one for me; but in the end, I wasn't and I was grateful. But I realized I had to stop testing God. When I redefined my definition of family from me, him, and the children, to me and the children and when the husband came along, then it would be me, Him, and the children but for that season in my life, I was complete with just me and my daughter. From that moment on, I continued to be involved in things that made me feel great about the woman God made me to be.

THIS IS NOW (2017)

It is now 2017 and I came to realize that God purposely had me single for as long as I was so that I could obtain the knowledge and information I am sharing with others. Every step of the way He was always there with me. Through every break up, through every volunteer and business opportunity I was involved in, God was always there. When I finished interviewing the bachelors, I knew I wanted to publish it as a book. Back then it was going to be called "The Black Man's Buffet" and I envisioned a buffet table with different women faces for the men to choose from. But over the years, I came to realize the issues with dating are not isolated to our race, or even the region of the country we live in. The challenges with communication have always existed because we haven't been taught as women that we need to learn how to become more effective with others when they are different from us. If what you are doing is working for you, then that is awesome. But if you feel like you are on the merry-go-round of crazy and if you could just get the information you need, you'd be willing to fix your situation, then this book and my other books in the Cake Chronicles 80/20 Healthy Relationship series is for you!

KEEP DOING

_____

_____

_____

_____

_____

_____

_____

START DOING

_____

_____

_____

_____

_____

STOP DOING

_____

_____

_____

_____

_____

MRS. DEBBIE'S REFLECTIONS

SUMMARY I
MRS. DEBBIE CAKES SUMMARY ABOUT THE BACHELORS

Even though I did not get the chance to ask all 70 questions to all of the bachelors, the questions that were answered provided me the foundation I needed to know about men. They are not necessarily cold, heartless, and calculating. They are just very analytical and a true "man's man" thinks in black and white. The majority of them don't like long, drawn out stories, and they really don't like to read. They are really simple, and yet at the same time "complicated." They are complicated to women because they do something most women have never learned they needed to learn how to do; and that is to read people. They study a person's mannerism to see if they are a person of their word, or if they are just users and manipulators. Women by human nature are nurturers and caretakers. They enjoy helping, and taking care of others, and many times they will take care of others over taking care of themselves. If they were raised or living in a dysfunctional household, they most likely were never given the permission to put their needs first and to take care of themselves. When you grow up as a child taking care of others, you become a woman who feels compelled to take care of others over yourself. Many women even find pleasure and joy taking care of others; however, they find themselves drained, and unappreciated. Men realize how women are and yet, until they are ready to be committed to someone, their need for conquest overshadows their ability to empathize and to be patient with their partner. Young boys are taught to be stingy with women. Many times they have even been instructed to use women to get what they want. Until women learn how to love themselves, define healthy boundaries for behavior that is not conducive for a healthy relationship, and then read and determine the behavior of the person in their life to see what boundaries may be needed for that relationship; we will continue to find many single, beautiful, young and older women living alone, wishing they were in a healthy relationship with a partner. The reason they will be single is because they have not been given the tools to determine if the person in their life compliments them, or not. Women no longer want to be used and abused for someone else's personal gain, but until they are willing to do the work to change their views and perceptions about communicating with others, they will continue to find themselves prey, and victimized by others. If we want to see a change in our men, we must first see the change in ourselves. We have to hold them to a higher standard, and because we are not doing that, they aren't. Like the bachelors said, they will continue having sex with a number of women until they find themselves "ready" to settle down. If you desire to establish a relationship with someone, you have to stop using sex as a prerequisite to getting to know them because in the end, you'll just be one more female they've had sex with that never really meant anything to them. I went into every "dating/relationship" situation trying to build something with them. Unfortunately, many times I purposely chose to date men who needed me more than I needed them. I was Ms. Fix it, and Ms. Rescuer. I had the house, car, insurance, and job. so they stepped into a readymade situation. However; after I met with my bachelors, I stopped being on the black man's buffet table and eventually found myself preparing for the man God was preparing for me.

SUMMARY II - MRS. DEBBIE CAKES – THE WIFE

When I was 18, I married my daughter's father but I knew when we dated that he was wounded and had relationship scars, but I thought my "love" for him could conquer anything. Since having interviewed the bachelors, I realized I needed to have a more in depth understanding about why relationships are toxic to the point that my grandmother could use a joke or a saying to define the process *"First Month Sugar, Second Month Pie, Third Month Go To Hell, Damn You, and Die!"* After the interviews with the bachelors I read 2 books; *Men Are From Mars, & Men Are From Venus*, and the *Five Love Languages*. After reading those books, I realized I had a very unhealthy view about dating, love, relationships and communicating with others so I started looking at my relationships with men, my daughter, my mother, my grandmother, my nieces, nephew, cousins, aunts, and my uncles. God then directed me to read another book called *The Victim Trap* which help to define dysfunction and the unhealthy behaviors that came from living in a controlling and toxic household. Those three books were great at putting me on the path to healthier communication skills; but I could still see there was still much more to learn. I later read the *Love Dare* and that book helped me understand that love **can be** defined, but we have to know how to ask the right questions in order to determine if the person in our life supports us, or if they don't, then we need to set boundaries because they will wound you. Once I realized the tools I needed to define a healthy, happy, long lasting relationship, I then realized I had to stop telling God what I wanted in a mate, because He already knew. If I trusted and believed in Him, then through my faith, I would trust and believe He would send me a man who was truly meant for me. In the fall of 2008 after being frustrated with my dating choices, I submitted my dating practices to Him. Once I did that, 30 days later in January 2009, I met Mr. Eddie Lee Brown Jr. On our first date, the Holy Spirit spoke to me and told me to calm down, relax, and just enjoy the process of getting to know who he was as a person, and not who he could be as a potential "husband." Trust and believe that even though I knew when I met him that he was the man God was preparing me for, without the knowledge that was shared with me by the bachelors, I would most likely still be single. My new communication skills were put to the test with my husband, my family, and our blended family. What I've learned is that women have to be willing to change. What you are changing is your "perception" about communicating with men and others. It is not that they won't change or be held accountable to change. The tricky part is for you to learn how to communicate with them in a way that gets the results you want. You have to be loving, supportive, firm, and still set boundaries. All of that is a lot of work, but when you master it with God's help and the Holy Spirit, you become a wife who is cherished and loved more than silver and gold. My husband spoils me, and I spoil him. He has grown significantly over the years because of me, and I have as well. I was the self sufficient, independent, all that and a bag of chips woman he met, and God graciously humbled me to realize I not only have a husband, but I have a partner, provider, and friend. He is what I needed, which in turn made him the man I wanted. The keys to a healthier happier relationship lies within you, and the pages of If I Can't Be The Cake, I won't be the Crumz!

SUMMARY III
NOW THAT YOU KNOW, WHAT ARE YOU GOING TO DO

Closing Points:
1. Require and embody the truth
2. What you can live with and without
3. Adapt now, and pay later
4. The joy of intimacy is the reward of commitment
5. The right thing at the wrong time is still the wrong thing
6. You'll never meet Mr. Right unless you're Mrs. Right
7. Starting over with a clean slate
8. How to make a man think about you all the time

My thoughts: two things men need to change:
1. Problems dating women who are sexually educated
2. Don't want their wives to be sexually educated

BUY MY OTHER BOOKS AVAILABLE ON AMAZON.COM

Adult Edition

Christian Edition

Teen Edition

www.ingramcontent.com/pod-product-compliance
Lightning Source LLC
Chambersburg PA
CBHW072207090426
42740CB00012B/2420